Cambridge Elements ≡

Elements in Eighteenth-Century Connections
edited by
Eve Tavor Bannet
University of Oklahoma
Rebecca Bullard
University of Reading

DISAVOWING DISABILITY

Richard Baxter and the Conditions of Salvation

Andrew McKendry
Nord University

CAMBRIDGE
UNIVERSITY PRESS

CAMBRIDGE
UNIVERSITY PRESS

University Printing House, Cambridge CB2 8BS, United Kingdom

One Liberty Plaza, 20th Floor, New York, NY 10006, USA

477 Williamstown Road, Port Melbourne, VIC 3207, Australia

314–321, 3rd Floor, Plot 3, Splendor Forum, Jasola District Centre, New Delhi – 110025, India

103 Penang Road, #05–06/07, Visioncrest Commercial, Singapore 238467

Cambridge University Press is part of the University of Cambridge.

It furthers the University's mission by disseminating knowledge in the pursuit of education, learning, and research at the highest international levels of excellence.

www.cambridge.org
Information on this title: www.cambridge.org/9781108823128
DOI: 10.1017/9781108913515

When citing this work, please include a reference to the DOI 10.1017/9781108913515

First published 2021

A catalogue record for this publication is available from the British Library.

ISBN 978-1-108-82312-8 Paperback
ISSN 2632-5578 (online)
ISSN 2632-556X (print)

Disavowing Disability

Richard Baxter and the Conditions of Salvation

Elements in Eighteenth-Century Connections

DOI: 10.1017/9781108913515
First published online: July 2021

Andrew McKendry
Nord University
Author for correspondence: Andrew McKendry, andrew.mckendry@nord.no

Abstract: *Disavowing Disability* examines the role that disability, both as a concept and an experience, played in seventeenth-century debates about salvation and religious practice. Exploring how the use and definition of the term "disability" functioned to allocate agency and culpability, this study argues that the post-Restoration imperative to capacitate "all men" – not just the "elect" – entailed a conceptual circumscription of disability, one premised on a normative imputation of capability. The work of Richard Baxter, sometimes considered a harbinger of 'modernity' and one of the most influential divines of the Long Eighteenth Century, elucidates this multifarious process of enabling. In constructing an ideology of ability that imposed moral self-determination, Baxter encountered a germinal form of the "problem" of disability in liberal theory. While a strategy of "inclusionism" served to assimilate most manifestations of alterity, melancholy presented an intractability that frustrated the logic of rehabilitation in fatal ways. This title is also available as Open Access on Cambridge Core.

This Element also has a video abstract: www.cambridge.org/mckendry

Keywords: disability, religion, liberalism, melancholy, Richard Baxter

ISBNs: 9781108823128 (PB), 9781108913515 (OC)
ISSNs: 2632-5578 (online), 2632-556X (print)

Contents

1 Introduction

From colonial classrooms to Allied trenches, the exploits of John Bunyan's redoubtable "Christian" have provided such a sedimented mythos of masculine self-mastery that we can easily forget how haphazard, even clumsy, his progress often is. For modern readers, plagued as we are with more despair than demonic foes, few episodes of *Pilgrim's Progress* seem so touch-and-go as his run-in with the "Giant Despair," a castle-doctrine landowner who pressures his despondent prisoners to kill themselves. After more than a week of starvation and beatings in the dungeon, Christian escapes improbably with a key he has had all along.[1] A simple pillar is erected to warn later travelers, but the burden of actually conquering Despair is left to the unlikely heroes of the undersung 1684 sequel: women, children, "halt," and "feebleminded." Though it is the superhuman Great-Heart who decapitates the giant, it is ultimately these "weakly" pilgrims who protect the reader from despair. As an updated pillar explains, any who doubt their deliverance from despair can find assurance in the (illustrated) dancing of "Ready-to-halt," who "could not dance without one Crutch in his Hand," but still "footed it well."[2] Along with his fellow traveler "Feeblemind," these "weak" pilgrims figure quite prominently in the narrative, explicitly serving to consecrate communal values such as care, companionship, and mutual accommodation. Neither rehabilitated nor cured, "Ready-to-halt" and "Feeblemind" attest to the fact, noted by scholars such as Lennard Davis and Kim Nielsen,[3] that cultural history abounds with disability, appearing as it does in poems, songs, diaries, letters, paintings, engravings, sermons, and even objects. As Douglas Baynton put it, "disability is everywhere in history, once you begin looking for it, but conspicuously absent in the histories we write."[4] Indeed, we need not look far for discussions of disability in Bunyan. He argued elsewhere that the transformative process of conversion emerged from disability – not just contrition or spiritual "trouble," but "a heart *disabled* . . . as a man whose bones are broken, is *disabled*, as to his way of running, leaping, [or] wrestling."[5]

The very deliberateness with which Bunyan connects "disability" to impairment,[6] however, reveals the quagmire that any history of disability encounters from the outset. The term had a different meaning in Bunyan's day

---

[1] Bunyan, *Pilgrim's Progress*, 150–154.   [2] Bunyan, *Second Part*, 181.
[3] Davis, *Enforcing*; Nielsen, *Disability History*.   [4] Baynton, "Inequality," 31.
[5] Bunyan, *Acceptable*, 45–46.
[6] The distinction between impairment – "a form of biological, cognitive, sensory or psychological difference that is defined often within a medical context" – and disability – "the negative social reaction" rooted in social structures – remains useful for marking the structural sources of injustice (Goodley, *Introduction*, 8), but it has been criticized for oversimplifying the complexities of embodiment and materiality.

than it does in our own, so modern notions of disability cannot be readily applied to discussing seventeenth-century experience. After all, Bunyan is promoting *spiritual* disability, and the impairments of his pilgrims are allegorical – connected with divine rather than social justice. But any attempt to reconstruct the ancestry of modern disability demands an investigation of such episodes, especially if we hope to identify what is so distinctive (and perhaps limited) about our own attitudes. Put simply, we cannot eschew such archives without missing what disability was and is. There is evidently more than mere nomenclature at stake here; the relevance of such sources, along with the broader role of historical research, hinge significantly on whether we can call premodern instances of "lameness," "infirmity," or even "disability" by the name of disability.

Taking this quagmire as its starting point, this Element explores how disability was conceptualized in seventeenth-century religious writing, in particular that of the influential divine Richard Baxter. Joining the ongoing (and contentious) debate about the ancestry of the concept, this Element aims to demonstrate how some of the essential groundwork for its later development was laid by theological shifts during this early period. I thus offer a prehistory of modern disability, one that complements and complicates conventional periodization by explicating some of the antecedents of the shifts that scholars typically foreground. Many of the features that usually signal a modern paradigm of disability, such as the ascendancy of medical authority and the dominion of industrial capitalism, were not yet established in Baxter's day. And that is partly the point here; *Disavowing Disability* examines the notions of "natural ability," human nature, and personal culpability that underlie later developments. The negotiation of such elemental categories, particularly through the social contract theory rooted in the seventeenth century, seminally informed the tradition of subjecthood, rights, and justice that we live with today. As theorists and activists now recognize, this tradition is profoundly problematized by disability, which represents an exception to the standards of rationality and autonomy that liberal theory, from Locke to Rawls, normally presumes. Baxter encountered analogues of this problem, both theoretical and practical, when he pursued his own reconfiguration of justice. His endeavor to capacitate "all men" under one standardized "law" jarred with the heterogeneity of the people he sought to compass. In elucidating this bind, I draw on theory from modern Disability Studies, as it illuminates the stakes that connect debates about disability across historical periods. Disability complicates our systems of categorization and discipline, so my approach necessarily transgresses disciplinary boundaries; Richard Baxter sits unusually alongside Judith Butler and Jasbir Puar. Lumbering across entrenched battle lines so optimistically is characteristic of Baxter himself, but I hope my own attempts at alliance-building are more successful, or at least less abrasive.

Unearthing the "ideology of ability"[7] broadly ascribed to the Enlightenment will require us to visit some archives of disability that are dated, daunting, or even dusty. While today fateful discussions about disability happen in policy documents, scientific journals, court decisions, and social media channels, in the early Enlightenment much of this discursive negotiation occurred in sermons, theological tracts, and moral guidebooks. Both as concept and as lived experience, disability was an important battleground in the epochal clash over Christian salvation: Who was saved? What faculties were involved in making them righteous? How should the Christian community be constituted and regulated? These questions represented foundational debates about divine justice and pastoral access, and their stakes overlap meaningfully with modern discussions about social justice and accessibility. The possibilities and challenges of engaging these debates through modern disability theory are examined in Section 2, "Contexts and Connections," which provides a critical overview of how religion has (and has not) figured in Disability Studies, as well as how recent research on secular embodiment has (and has not) attended to disability. Foregrounding the filiations between the histories of ableism and secularism, I suggest in this section, could enhance our understanding of not only Baxter, but also the norms of embodiment and personhood established by the Enlightenment.

The 'Enlightenment,' of course, was not a monolithic entity, nor was early Enlightenment 'religion.' As Section 3, "Enabling 'Every Man,'" demonstrates, shifts in the landscape of seventeenth-century theology altered the role and implications that "disability" held in religious thought. The Calvinistic theology that defined the first half of the century emphasized the depravity and utter impotence engendered by the Fall, such that "disability" was regularly considered the "natural" and universal state of humankind. In the decades that followed the Civil War, however, England witnessed a far-reaching transformation of Reformed theology, salvation being increasingly offered on conditions and performance, rather than as a gratuitous gift. This shift entailed a variegated process of what I call soteriological enabling, significantly modifying the theological and moral definition of "disability"; by the early eighteenth century, the term became far less commonly used to describe the universal limitations of postlapsarian humankind, which allowed it to more firmly demarcate exceptional incapacities that deviated from "ordinary" life. From this angle, the "decline" of Calvinism involved not simply an exaltation of "natural faculties," most notably reason, but also a pathologization of "disability." As the idea that "disability" was the "natural" or inevitable state of the postlapsarian person

---

[7] Siebers, *Disability Theory*, 7.

went out of fashion, the category became (particularly in religious writing) the differentiating rather than defining character of humankind.

There was perhaps no writer more entangled in this reconfiguration than Richard Baxter, the protean divine – 'puritan,' 'liberal,' 'moderate,' 'heretic' – who intervened in the theology of the age so provocatively.[8] Section 4, "Disputing Disability, Conditioning Salvation," turns to his voluminous oeuvre, examining his efforts to redefine and regulate the concept of disability. Driven at once by fears of social collapse and hopes of universal harmony, Baxter propagated a theology that extended the promise of redemption to "all men" – on certain conditions. Put simply, he declared that no one was disabled. This redistribution of salvific agency entailed a normative imputation of universal capability: Every person had the potential to be saved because they possessed the "natural faculties" necessary to do their part. To maintain the integrity and justice of this schema, Baxter had to disavow and circumscribe disability so that nobody, whether "reprobate" or "lame," could be constitutionally excluded from the laws of salvation. In defining and defending this system against criticisms and alternatives, Baxter channels a telling dissonance: Faced with impairment – in his readers, his parishioners, even himself – he could not significantly abrogate the demands of capability, even (or perhaps most of all) when they seemed unfair, impossible, or even cruel. In presuming ability so relentlessly and imperiously, Baxter's theology was "ableist" in the sense theorized by modern Disability Studies. But this framing serves less as an indictment than as an invitation to explore why Baxter was so anxious about the exceptions disability represented. Since this tension emerged from his naturalization of a presumptively capable theo-political subject, the bind Baxter encountered can be seen as an early expression of a "problem" inherent to the liberal paradigm rooted in this period: Persons with disabilities were disadvantaged or excluded in adverse ways by the very mechanisms that otherwise promised inclusion and liberty.

As Section 5, "Diversity, Inclusion(ism), Discipline," argues, the imperative to regulate "disability" was entirely consistent with a strategy of "inclusionism" that recognized, even celebrated, human variability and vulnerability. Though his touting of 'diversity' often served to impugn the Established Church (from which he reluctantly dissented), Baxter's sensitivity to physiological differences was reflected in his vision of education, church membership, and health care. These systems had to be finely adjusted to the irreducible heterogeneity of humankind. Implementing a sufficiently differentiated system, however, was tellingly complicated. Baxter's attempts to tailor support to every member

---

[8] On Baxter's life and thought: Boersma, *Pepper Corn*; Cooper, *Formation*; Keeble, *Puritan*; Lamont, *Millennium*; Rivers, *Reason*, 89–163; Sytsma, *Mechanical Philosophers*.

illustrate how the potential injustice of conditioning salvation inhered in the scalar gaps between an ideology of ability and everyday care. These gaps are particularly apparent with respect to intellectual disability, which Baxter encountered in relation to "idiocy." Though he refused to explicitly exclude "ideots" from salvation, since this would compromise its universality, they were rendered socially invisible by his procedures of community membership. In this sense, he had recourse to the same techniques of deferral that still define liberal responses to intellectual disability, particularly in educational contexts.

For personal and polemical reasons, Baxter was unable to so defer the problem of melancholy. This impasse occupies the final section, "Melancholy, Means, Ends," partly because it haunted Baxter and partly because it still haunts us. Rooted in theological conflicts of the seventeenth century yet resonating far beyond his age, this problem was at once plain and perplexing: A vast swathe of "all men" seemed to be legitimately "disabled" by melancholy, yet this was systemically inadmissible. While Baxter affirmed that melancholics, living as they did under the same "law" as "all men," necessarily retained their moral capability and culpability, his accounts of their experience tell a more compli- cated and implicating story. As he discovered so variously and tragically, the problem with melancholy was that it frustrated all discursive means and methods, focalizing the violence that remained, in the final instance, at the foundation of his theo-political framework. Probing the systemic boundaries exposed by melancholics provides an occasion to think about how far a system of justice premised on capability might go, as well as what collateral damage its procedures and practices might cause.

Baxter's own attempts at plainness spawned tomes of tangled logic, so it is worth announcing our promised destination now, before detours and disputa- tions draw us off track: This Element argues that Baxter's response to disability, particularly as it troubled his ableist soteriology, represents an important moment in the theological prehistory of disability, exposing some of the con- ceptual problems that continue to haunt the liberal tradition of justice.

2 Contexts and Connections

Disavowing Disability connects two traditionally separate topics of study: dis- ability and secularism. The differentiation of "disability" examined here emerged from trends that critical reassessments of secularism have made visible. Yet, the most profound consequence of secularization – its impact on paradigms of personhood – can only be fully understood through the frameworks developed in Disability Studies, since they explore alternatives that persist here and now. A rapprochement of these seemingly discordant fields suggests that they are

excavating, albeit with different tools, the same historical process: The normative
"ableism" bequeathed by the Enlightenment emerged from the process of secularization, particularly the antiquation of high Calvinist "disability."

Reconstructing the history of disability has been among the most integral
endeavors of Disability Studies, but also perhaps the most complicated and
contentious. Whether highlighting alterity or continuity, investigations of disability have revealed how distinctive and contingent is our 'modern' conception of
disability; the meaning and implications of disability differ enormously across
periods and cultures. This recognition, evidenced and enriched with period- and
case-oriented studies, has helped denaturalize many modern assumptions about
disability, illustrating that they are not inevitable or universal. But while the
distinctiveness of modern notions is regularly invoked, there remains abiding
disagreement about its periodization: When exactly did this 'modern' paradigm
take form? Many scholars, such as Lennard Davis and Rosemarie Garland-
Thomson,[9] have anchored this shift in the nineteenth century, and broad historical
studies of disability, such as *Disability Histories*,[10] typically reflect this periodization in their focus. A constellation of current research, however, situates this
shift significantly earlier – in the seventeenth and eighteenth centuries. The
pioneering *Recovering Disability in Early Modern England* is premised on the
idea that "'disabled' was indeed an operational identity category in the English
Renaissance," and Elizabeth Bearden has recently contended that "early modern
people were working with many of the same discourses of disability and embodiment that we engage now."[11] These projects have not lacked historical accuracy
and rigor; dating 'modern' disability is partly a matter of conscious emphasis,
hinging on which elements of disability are foregrounded. Whereas privileging
topics like medicine and statistics pulls our attention to the nineteenth century,
foregrounding issues like stigmatization and institutionalization often points us to
earlier developments.

For studies of disability focused on notions of personhood and rights, the
seventeenth century is an indisputable foundation. Prevailing conceptions of
rationality are rooted in the philosophy that emerged from this period, as are our
attendant definitions of human nature and species-membership. For better or
worse, the tenets of philosophers like Descartes and Hobbes continue to inform
debates about disability, both directly and indirectly via modern thinkers like
John Rawls, Amartya Sen, and David Gauthier. Theorists of disability have
often invoked the legacy of the Enlightenment in broad strokes, noting how its

[9] Davis, *Enforcing*; Garland-Thomson, *Extraordinary*.
[10] Burch and Rembis (eds.), *Histories*.
[11] Hobgood and Wood (eds.), *Recovering*, 7; Bearden, *Monstrous Kinds*, 75. Also, Love, *Theatre*; Williams, "Enabling."

definitive "optimism about the rationality and autonomy of man"[12] cast disability in a new role – as the boundary or exception to rational personhood.[13] The precise details of this epochal "ableism," particularly as it emerged from early Enlightenment political theory, are now being more finely articulated by scholars like Stacy Clifford Simplican and Barbara Arneil, who have variously demonstrated how social contract theory "bases political membership on a threshold level of capacity and excludes anyone who falls below."[14] From this perspective, the liberal tradition proffers a "capacity contract" or "ableist contract" that incidentally or even integrally excludes persons with disabilities from the domain of justice.[15] As Martha Nussbaum has argued, these inherent biases of social contract theory leave disability as an "unsolved problem of justice" in the liberal tradition,[16] one that we can trace back to its origins in writers like Locke and Kant.

However pragmatic or precise our approach to the topic, any study of disability that makes transhistorical connections is confronted with a lexicographic quagmire as deep and daunting as the Slough of Despond: The definition of disability was not the same in seventeenth-century English, so premodern instances of impairment cannot be called "disability" in any straightforward or unqualified way. As such, studies of premodern disability have usually focused on discourses of "deformity," "monstrosity," and "defect,"[17] which provide more coherent categories than "disability." Premodern writers did use the word "disability," but were they really talking about disability in any sense commensurate with our own? Though the term *was* sometimes used to characterize the effects of bodily impairment, it was also enlisted to describe various other forms of incapacity; we find individuals disabled by injury and defect, but many others are "disabled" by financial or legal incapacity, by poverty and policy.[18] Well into the nineteenth century, the term "disability" was used in ways that cannot be cleanly aligned with our own,

---

[12] Campbell, "Ability," 12.

[13] Erevelles, *Difference*, 29–30. Also, Garland-Thomson, *Extraordinary*, 38–40; Siebers, *Disability Theory*, 93–94.

[14] Simplican, *Capacity Contract*, 27; Arneil, "Self Image." On disability as a "problem" for liberal theory: Arneil and Hirschmann (eds.), *Political Theory*; Ball, "Autonomy"; Barclay, *Dignity*; Breckenridge and Vogler, "Limits"; Davidson, *Concerto*; Hirschmann, "Freedom and (Dis) Ability"; "Disability Rights"; Kittay, "Ethics"; Kittay and Carlson (eds.), *Cognitive*; Nussbaum, *Frontiers*; Riddle (ed.), *Theory to Practice*; Silvers and Francis, "Justice"; Wong, "Duties."

[15] Pinheiro, "Ableist Contract"; Simplican, *Capacity Contract*.   [16] Nussbaum, *Frontiers*, 3.

[17] Classen (ed.), *Old Age*; Deutsch and Nussbaum (eds.), *Defects*; Garland, *Beholder*; Garland-Thomson (ed.), *Freakery*; Knoppers and Landes (eds.), *Monstrous Bodies*; Metzler, *Middle Ages*; Singer, "Social Body"; Turner and Stagg (eds.), *Social Histories*; Wood, "Staging."

[18] For definitions of "disability" in seventeenth- and eighteenth-century writing: Nelson and Alker, "Perfect," 33–34; Turner, *Eighteenth-Century*, 16–34.

as Essaka Joshua has recently argued.[19] Jeffrey Wilson has contended that this conceptual disjunct undermines projects (such as the 2009 "Disabled Shakespeares" special edition of *Disability Studies Quarterly*) that claim to uncover modern "disability" in early modern writing.[20] When I have taught units and classes on seventeenth- and eighteenth-century disability, students have eagerly compared our own various experiences of impairment (such as hearing impairment, in my case) with those we are reading about – from John Milton, Sarah Scott, or William Hay. Such meaningful resonances may tempt us to disregard the nomenclature of "disability" as a mere philological quibble, but it is more instructive – for students and scholars – to unpack the semantic complexities of the term as it was used in the seventeenth century. The fact that the word disability was far more context-dependent, describing incapacity in relation to specific circumstances (often not bodily), occasions queries that can denaturalize its modern meaning: How is being disabled for military service different than being disabled for domestic labor? How did civil disability, as was the fate of Dissenters under the Clarendon Code, relate to the legal disability experienced by "ideots" and "lunatics"? If disability is socially mediated, how is being disabled by poverty connected with being disabled by injury? Precisely because we *cannot* treat seventeenth-century "disability" as a monolithic category of identity or experience, it is all the more worthwhile to carefully investigate the discursive fields in which it possessed specific meanings. This may point us toward fields, terms, and topics we might not expect; whereas today medical discourse draws the most attention in studies of disability, seventeenth-century tenets about the extent and character of human ability were rooted far more deeply in religious discourse – in accounts of the Fall, notions of providence, and ideas of divine order. Before the cultural ascendancy of doctors and medical technology, it was religious writers who were often debating and determining what humans were capable of physically, mentally, and morally. Though the occasions for these debates may seem alien or immaterial to our own age, the attendant discussions about the dynamics of ability frequently entailed the same fundamental concerns as we have today: the boundaries of community, the ethics of accommodation, the nature of justice, and the commensurability of human experience.

Unpacking the ramifications of such an archive, however, will arguably require a more fine-grained account of religion than we currently use in studying disability. Though scholarship on the connections between religion and disability is expanding, generalized conceptualizations of 'Christianity' (not to mention 'religion' more broadly) have typically inhibited historically and

---

[19] Joshua, *Physical*, 1.   [20] Wilson, "Trouble."

analytically nuanced treatments of those connections. Despite the 'turn to religion' in both historiography and theory, Disability Studies remains a conspicuously secular field. Monographs and collections, such as the ambitious *Disability and Social Theory* or the well-established *Disability Studies Reader*,[21] feature little to no engagement with religion,[22] and the otherwise thorough *Keywords for Disability Studies* moves right from "rehabilitation" to "representation."[23] As Shaun Grech suggests, the marked absence of religion in Disability Studies is "symptomatic of the broader secularism" that permeates such scholarship,[24] a trend apparent not only in topics of study but also in the way religion is imagined. Whereas disability emerges (quite rightly) as a complex and culturally inflected locus of identity and experience, religion regularly functions as little more than an inert set of cultural norms or dicta. This tendency is rooted in the disciplinary position and history of Disability Studies,[25] which coalesced around methodologies, particularly Marxism and identity politics, that have been characteristically antipathetic to religion in many modalities. As such, the 'religious model' of disability has traditionally appeared oppressive and backward even in comparatively intersectional approaches to disability. More recent correctives to this trend, such as *Disability and Religious Diversity*,[26] have indicated how important religion, in all its lived complexity, might be to the history of disability. Historical and comparative studies, such as Saul Olyan's *Disability in the Hebrew Bible*, have uncovered the cultural contingency of notions like "wholeness" and "defect,"[27] while disability-oriented theology, most notably Amos Yong's *Theology and Down Syndrome*, has challenged the ableism inherited by modern Christianity.[28]

Yet, partly because such research has been breaking new ground, the consequences of more localized historical shifts have been almost entirely neglected, such that arguments about concepts like 'sin' or 'punishment' are often detached from the particular circumstances in which they were contested and experienced. This generalized approach is especially ill-suited to seventeenth-century England, a moment at which the very definition of Christianity,

---

[21] Davis (ed.), *Reader*; Goodley et al. (eds.), *Social Theory*.

[22] On this trend: Creamer, "Theological Accessibility"; Imhoff, "Religion"; Tomalin, "Rights-Based."

[23] Adams et al. (eds.), *Keywords*.   [24] Grech, "Majority," 64.

[25] On the history of the field: Burch and Sutherland, "Not Yet Here"; Garland, *Beholder*; Hall, *Literature*, 19–29; Hughes, *Invalidity*; Kudlick, "Disability History"; Rembis et al. (eds.), *Handbook*; Stiker, *History*.

[26] Schumm and Stoltzfus (eds.), *Diversity*.

[27] Olyan, *Hebrew Bible*; Schipper, *Hebrew Bible*; Schumm and Stoltzfus (eds.), *Sacred Texts*; Wheatley, *Stumbling Blocks*.

[28] Yong, *Theology*. Also, Eiesland, *Disabled God*; Reynolds, *Vulnerable*.

including its fundamental structures and practices, was thrown into question. When persons with disabilities were excluded from communion, for instance, did this reflect on 'Christianity,' on 'Protestantism,' on a specific sect, a specific controversy, or even a specific minister? Seventeenth-century scuffles over sacraments and church government may sometimes look irrelevant or even quaint to modern scholars of disability, but they had a far-reaching impact on Enlightenment thought and policy. What is often broadly imagined as the 'Enlightenment model' of disability emerged from the exigencies, concessions, and outcomes these localized struggles yielded.

While repositioning disability at the center of historical analysis might alter our account of Enlightenment philosophy and political theory, such a reorientation could also enrich our understanding of the secular condition we have inherited – its origins and limitations. The classical 'secularization thesis,' which asserted that religion was inexorably declining in cultural importance, has long been dethroned both by revisionist historiography and political theory.[29] But the extent to which modern experience is nevertheless mediated by secularity is only now coming into focus. Whether refurbishing or renouncing secularism, recent discussions have revealed that secularity reaches far beyond institutions and policies, engendering a mode of embodiment defined by self-reflexivity, impermeability, and continence. In renovations of secularism,[30] this is reflected in the "epistemic stance" enjoined by Jürgen Habermas or the "autonomy" sanctified by Will Kymlicka.[31] In critical treatments of secularism (sometimes labeled "postsecular"), the "buffered" self deconstructed by Charles Taylor is the most prominent touchstone,[32] but a number of theorists have suggested more specifically that the "secular body" is defined by its distinctive relationship to injury and pain – mediated, partitioned, insulated.[33] This is partly why Talal Asad has suggested that secularism might be most fully understood by querying its norms of embodiment: "How do attitudes to the human body (to pain, physical damage, decay, and death, to physical integrity, bodily growth, and sexual enjoyment) differ in various forms of life? What

---

[29] For established critiques: Balibar, *Cosmopolitanism*; Berger (ed.), *Desecularization*; Casanova, *Public*; Fessenden, *Redemption*; Keane, "Secularism?"; Stark, "Secularization, RIP"; Warner, *Secularization*.

[30] Butler et al., *Public Sphere*; Calhoun et al. (eds.), *Rethinking*; Ghosh (ed.), *Sense*; Habermas, "Religion"; "Notes"; Maclure and Taylor, *Secularism*; Stout, *Democracy*; Warner et al. (eds.), *Varieties*; Zuckerman and Shook (eds.), *Handbook*.

[31] Habermas, "Religion"; Kymlicka, *Citizenship*.

[32] Taylor, *Secular Age*. Also, Abeysekara, *Politics*; Bilgrami, *Enchantment*; Fraser, "Rethinking"; Sandel, "Procedural."

[33] Asad, "Secular Body"; Hirschkind, "Secular Body?"; Mahmood, "Secular Affect"; Scheer et al. (eds.), *Secular Bodies*.

structures of the senses – hearing, seeing, touching – do these attitudes depend on?"[34]

Disability raises such questions in most insistent and distinctive ways, so it is remarkable that the issue is almost entirely absent from accounts of secularism. Whether construed through phenomenology or Marxist theory, disability challenges the core concepts of liberal society, disrupting "the illusion of autonomy, self-government, and self-determination that underpins the fantasy of absolute able-bodiedness."[35] Disability Studies has recuperated forms of porousness and "leaky[ness]" that belie the "buffered" self of secularity.[36] Historicizations of autonomy and "normalcy" have defamiliarized assumptions about experience that scholars like Mahmood and Asad have sought to interrogate.[37] If secularity inheres not simply in policies and laws but more elementally in forms of embodiment, then the structures of ableism elucidated by scholars like Campbell and Erevelles might be considered foundational to secularity.[38] How is it, then, that the search for what Taylor calls "a voice which we could never have assumed ourselves"[39] has not involved thinkers like Nancy Eiesland or Helen Betenbaugh,[40] whose experience of religion has been uniquely shaped by their experience of disability? This methodological lacuna is a consequence of approach: Privileging more generalizable forms of pain, like injury or trauma, facilitates broad cultural and historical comparisons in a way that the specificity of disability does not. Though such comparisons have helped expose the contingency of 'Western' ideas of personhood and suffering, they also reproduce a presumptive exaltation of capability that is at odds with attempts to unsettle secular embodiment. The fact that analysis of secularism has stalled here is no surprise; as Lennard Davis and Tobin Siebers have pointed out, even the most progressive projects have endorsed an "able body," either as an implicit norm or emancipatory ideal.[41] While we might censure Charles Taylor for so casually denigrating disability,[42] it may be more productive to examine how such implicit ableism precludes a more penetrating interrogation of concepts like choice and belief. Whether we are pursuing a nuanced reconsideration or a "destabilizing overhaul of first principles,"[43] any approach to secularism will have to reckon with the methodological ableism it has inherited.

While a traditionally disciplined history of either topic might foreground familiar figures such as Descartes or Locke, a transdisciplinary history of

---

[34] Asad, *Formations*, 17.   [35] Garland-Thomson, *Extraordinary*, 46.
[36] Shildrick, *Leaky*; Goodley and Runswick-Cole, "Possibility."
[37] Davis, *Enforcing*; Metzler, *Middle Ages*; Stiker, *History*.
[38] Campbell, *Contours*; Erevelles, *Difference*.   [39] Taylor, *Secular Age*, 754.
[40] Eiesland, *Disabled God*; Betenbaugh, "Lived Theology."
[41] Davis, *Enforcing*, 5, 27–28; Siebers, *Disability Theory*, 70–95.   [42] Arneil, "Self Image."
[43] Coviello and Hickman, "Introduction," 647.

disability and secularism – or perhaps a unified history of the "secular body" –
conjures up an oddly amphibious figure: Richard Baxter. By virtue of disciplinary divides as much as of his own eclecticism, Baxter is sprinkled across
established fields. He is suited to the history of both science and theology, and
we might find him in literary studies as readily as in philosophy or economic
history. In his own lifetime, his ambit was vast; he corresponded and visited
with natural philosophers like Robert Boyle and Henry More,[44] political theorists like Sir Matthew Hale,[45] and, of course, godly men such as William Penn
and James Ussher.[46] His thought was substantially informed by international
currents, among them Dutch and French theology, and his works were promptly
translated into French, German, and "Indian language" (i.e. Massachusett).[47]
His theology influenced prominent Christian worthies like Philip Doddrige,
John Wesley, and even C. S. Lewis.[48] But it was his 'practical' writings, such as
The Saints Everlasting Rest, which made him a household name in the centuries
that followed. The afterlife of such guides, celebrated by reformers like Johnson
and mocked by humorists like Twain,[49] shaped English colonialism, class
politics, and print culture in ways that are only now becoming clear.[50]

    With a finger in so many pies, Baxter has naturally served as a harbinger in
established narratives of secular modernity. His most influential role was as the
representative "Puritan" in Max Weber's *Protestant Ethic and the Spirit of
Capitalism*, in which he exemplifies the disciplined asceticism that legitimated
a new way of life. He subsequently came to figure as such in narratives of
modernization and secularization, among them the ascendancy of "rationalism,"
the "rise of moralism," and the establishment of deism.[51] Historians have regularly characterized Baxter as "a transitional figure between the old-style
Reformed Orthodoxy and the theology of the age of the Enlightenment," arguing
that his rationalistic Puritanism "prepares for life in a more tolerant age."[52] The
distortions of such broad-brush characterizations have been exposed by detailed
studies of Baxter, such as those by Hans Boersma and Simon Burton.[53] But these
welcome correctives have necessarily eschewed broader claims about his

---

[44] Letters 657, 720, 721, 764, 1091, 1102, 1115 in Keeble and Nuttall, *Calendar*. All subsequent
   references to Baxter's correspondence (excepting the Morris letter) are from this collection and
   will be cited by letter number (L#).
[45] L901A; L994; L1041.   [46] L961; L979–986; Baxter, *Reliquiae*, I.110, I.206.
[47] Baxter, *Saint Matthieu*; *Wehkomaonganoo*; *Ewige Ruhe*.
[48] Cunningham, "Justification"; Keeble, "C. S. Lewis"; Nuttall, *Doddridge*.
[49] Boswell, *Life*, I.110, II.457, II.477; Twain, "Advice," 566.
[50] Glickman, "Protestantism"; Keeble and Whitehouse, "Rewriting"; Round, *Removable*, 32–36.
[51] For representations of Baxter as a "proto-rationalist," "liberal" moralist, or progenitor of deism:
   Allison, *Rise*, 154–177; Gordon, *Heads*, 56–101; Nuttall et al., *Beginnings*, 48–60.
[52] Trueman, "Unity," 70; Damrosch, *God's Plot*, 56.
[53] Boersma, *Pepper Corn*; Burton, *Hallowing*.

relationship to modernity, so that Baxter remains strangely "underappreciated in the wider literature on the early Enlightenment" even as we know more than ever about his theology.[54] Few would now treat him as a mere mouthpiece of the "Protestant ethic," but his readers, both laudatory and critical, regularly affirm that he marked a sea change in systems of morality, discipline, and subjectivity. In what ways, then, did his thought, in all its particularity and idiosyncrasy, contribute to the modern project?

If secular liberalism is built around a presumptively able-bodied political subject, then it is arguably through his conception of disability that Baxter most significantly shaped modern thought. As his critics both in our century and his own have noted, Baxter proffered a theology that exalted human agency. J. I. Packer, perhaps his most eminent interlocutor, concluded that Baxter's rationalism "sowed the seeds of moralism with regard to sin, Arianism with regard to Christ, legalism with regard to faith and salvation, and liberalism with regard to God."[55] While it may be a stretch to charge Baxter, as M. H. MacKinnon does, with single-handedly killing "Calvin's omnipotent deity" and replacing Him with an "anthropocentric system of worship,"[56] he undeniably reduced many elements of religion to the level of human ability, legibility, and instrumentality. It was in this context – bringing divine justice to the level of man – that Baxter wrote extensively about disability, not only as it related to his own numerous illnesses, but also as it concerned friends and family, parishioners and patients, sin and salvation, church and state. In the *longue durée*, his reconceptualization of disability was evidently part of the broader movements in which he participated, among them the legitimation of voluntarism, the establishment of a disciplinary society, and the development of humanistic ethics. Yet, from such a distance it is impossible to see how integrally, and sometimes counterintuitively, disability figured in his relationship to these developments. His derogation of disability was bound up with his experience of the Civil War, and his attachment to discipline yielded an 'inclusive' attitude toward physiological difference. In his political and philosophical character, "none of the usual classifications of opinion or allegiance will apply,"[57] and the same might be said for his conceptualization of disability. When Baxter has figured in histories of illness and disability, his idiosyncrasy has been reduced to fit him within longer trends. He sometimes appears as a transitional figure in studies of melancholy, most notably in the work of Jeremy Schmidt, where he stands as an "anti-Calvinist" with a "strongly condemnatory, even cynical,

[54] Sytsma, *Mechanical Philosophers*, 8.   [55] Packer, *Quest*, 159–160.
[56] MacKinnon, "Calvinism," 163.   [57] Keeble, "Introduction," xiv.

attitude" toward melancholy.[58] In C. F. Goodey's sweeping history of intelligence, Baxter occupies a similar position, his exaltation of intelligence influencing the development of the modern concept of "intellectual disability"; by endorsing "intellectual development for all," Baxter helped make "idiocy" a necessary category.[59] I am happily indebted to such scholarship, which has fruitfully suggested how Baxter has shaped our modern perspectives. *Disavowing Disability*, however, focuses on his broader definition of "disability," which underpinned his responses to specific conditions like "melancholy" and "idiocy," as well as on his strategies of inclusion (and their shortcomings), which were arguably his most important contribution to the history of disability. Engaging the historical particularities of Baxter's worldview through modern theory allows us to treat his motivations charitably while still seeing their implications critically.

The critical perspectives from Disability Studies help us to articulate how the "anthropocentric" character of Baxter's thought forged a specific conception of the human, one that imposed capability and concomitantly denigrated disability. Reassessments of early modern philosophy are now beginning to draw quite productively on Disability Studies, connecting seventeenth-century writing with concepts like "ableism" and "cripping." Making such connections with a divine like Baxter is admittedly unusual, but there is no reason to exempt religious writing from theoretical scrutiny, nor to assume divines were any less sophisticated or influential. Baxter aspired to speak to readers of future ages, and his writing indeed continues to inform pastoral practices, popular Christianity, and self-help writing. But he was an essentially pragmatic man, and he might have fairly asked: What is actually gained by discussing his theology in modern terms? Describing his theology in relation to "ableism," as I do in this Element, points us to a set of dynamics and consequences that well-worn keywords – 'rationalism,' 'Arminianism,' or 'orthodoxy' – simply do not. Ableism typically describes those "ideas, practices, institutions, and social relations that presume able-bodiedness, and by so doing, construct persons with disabilities as marginalised, oppressed, and largely invisible 'others.'"[60] Though this systemic bias is most often traced to the built environment, theorists like Fiona Kumari Campbell and Jay Dolmage have shown that it can inhere in everyday metaphors, institutional policies, and narrative conventions.[61] Baxter's theology was "ableist" in "presum[ing] able-bodiedness" and in imposing a uniform law premised on this presumption.

[58] Schmidt, *Melancholy*, 103, 117–118. Also, Lund, *Melancholy*, 124–125; MacDonald, "Psychological Healing," 110–117; Rubin, *Religious Melancholy*, 33–37.
[59] Goodey, *Intelligence*, 96.
[60] Chouinard, "Making Space," 380. For other definitions: Campbell, *Contours*; Goodley, *Dis/ability*; Wolbring, "Ableism."
[61] Campbell, *Contours*; Dolmage, *Ableism*.

Indeed, his sanctification of rationality and self-determination has long been acknowledged by religious historians and theologians, and in this sense "ableism" is a different angle on recognized features of his thought. But this framing underlines an alternative legacy and logic to his oeuvre, situating him in the conceptual history of "compulsory able-bodiedness" and highlighting how his thought was connected across levels – from the abstractly theological to the prosaically pastoral – by a normative notion of "natural ability." The concept of the "normate," developed by Rosemarie Garland-Thomson, helps articulate how this systemic presumption of capability coalesced around a distinctive paradigm of personhood. The "normate" describes a "social figure," demarcated in opposition to deviant bodies, "through which people can represent themselves as definitive human beings."[62] This locution captures the stakes of species-membership that undergird Baxter's formulation of "all men," as well as the discursive circulation of this model; the role that Baxter proffered was a standardizing "subject position"[63] that all readers, regardless of their heterogeneity, were impelled to adopt or 'pass' for, often by abjuring the "exceptional" or "extraordinary." To be sure, these theoretical concepts cannot be imposed on seventeenth-century writing uncritically, and we will see where they are unseasonable. But they are hardly incompatible with seventeenth-century religion, not least because these divines were thinking through the problems and practicalities of justice far more carefully and earnestly than we usually imagine.

3 Enabling "Every Man"

Since seventeenth-century religious writing has furnished provocative challenges to capitalist and patriarchal worldviews both in its own day and in modern theory,[64] its absence from Disability Studies is quite remarkable; at a moment when the whole world was being turned upside down, established norms of ability and disability were being disrupted or even discarded in instructive ways. Disability figured significantly in the multifarious conflict that ruptured early Enlightenment England, featuring in debates about predestination, ecclesiology, communion, liturgy, baptism, and even toleration. As Disability Studies scholars have demonstrated, schemas of ritual and worship necessarily assume norms of capability that are problematized by disability.[65] The explosive reformation of established practices that defined the seventeenth century brought much of this problematization to the fore. From Levellers to Laudians, antithetical conceptions of personhood and community were floated

---

[62] Garland-Thomson, *Extraordinary*, 8.   [63] Ibid., 8–9.
[64] Apetrei, *Women*; Hill, *Upside Down*; Holstun, *Dagger*.
[65] Carter, *Including*; Gilman, "Sacrifice"; Pearson, "Rites."

and fought over. Even for those of us unfamiliar with the intricacies of seven-teenth-century sectarianism, it is not difficult to imagine the questions that intersected disability and religion at such a moment of contentious reconfigur-ation: What degree of comprehension and consent is necessary for baptism (and how do intellectual disabilities complicate such dynamics)? What competence and capacities are requisite for an "able" minister (and what impairments disqualified a minister from service)? How should communion be conducted (and how accessible should it be to disabled participants)? Though our own investment in these questions may emerge from a different set of priorities than those of Anglican bishops or Baptist preachers, such issues illustrate how disability functions as a transhistorical and transdisciplinary matter of justice and access.

As with all responses to disability, these disputes – say, over the baptism of "ideots" or the "fencing" of the communion table – reflected paradigms of capability that reached far beyond a single practice or occurrence. The meaning and status of disability played an important role in the stream of Calvinistic theology that defined England during the first half of the seventeenth century.[66] Fed by continental currents and hardened by clashes with Arminianism, this theology was characterized by its distinctive emphasis on gratuitous grace, predestined election (and reprobation), and limited atonement. Such doctrines severely depreciated human agency, which was considered largely (often abso-lutely) inconsequential in comparison to the meritorious agency of Christ. Broadly put, the individual themselves was utterly powerless to cause, deserve, or even influence their salvation. While this meant free salvation for the predestined elect, it also meant inalterable damnation for the reprobate: "let them doe what they will," the Anglican Churchman John Yates pronounced, "all shall be nought, pray or not pray, sacrifice or not sacrifice, come to church or not come to church."[67] In its most pronounced forms, this theology manifested as antinomianism, the view that Christians were not even bound to follow the moral law. Antinomians glorified a form of salvation given "on no condition, no performance at all."[68]

---

[66] There is some debate as to exactly how "Calvinist" this theology was, but many scholars now agree, pace Richard Muller (*Post-Reformation*), that the theology of the early seventeenth century was broadly consistent with the thought of Calvin. This historiographic stance is often signaled by the term "Reformed Orthodoxy"; I use "Calvinist" here simply because it is more familiar to a multidisciplinary readership. On the complexities of the "rise": Collinson, *Protestants*; Kendall, *Calvin*; Muller, *Calvin*; Trueman, "Reformed Orthodoxy"; Tyacke, *Anti-Calvinists*; "Counter-Revolution"; Wallace, *Predestination*; Webster, *Godly Clergy*.

[67] Yates, *Arraignement*, 276.

[68] Walwyn, *Power*, 31. On seventeenth-century antinomianism: Como, *Spirit*; Cooper, *Fear*; Hall, *Controversy*; Hessayon and Finnegan (eds.), *Varieties*.

The demotion of human agency that characterized Calvinist soteriology was defined by the language of impairment, including "disability." If disability functioned as an 'operative category' anywhere in seventeenth-century thought, it did so in such theological, homiletic, and moral writing, where it served regularly to describe the universal incapacity of postlapsarian humans. Divines like Thomas Gataker, George Downame, and James Ussher used the term in this way.[69] It also figured so in confessions of Reformed doctrine, most notably the Westminster Confession and the Savoy Declaration, which said that man was "utterly indisposed, dis-abled, and made opposite to all good."[70] The "utter disability of our nature, to doe any good" was a cornerstone of the Calvinist worldview.[71] The idea that disability was universal and natural is certainly surprising when compared with the "compulsory able-bodiedness" that defines heteronormative identity today.[72] Seventeenth-century Calvinism, however, represents no homogenous or practicable alternative; the claim that 'we are all disabled'[73] would have struck contemporaries as both banal and contentious, since the precise nature of this universal disability was a matter of intense debate. Though often associated offhandedly with Puritanism, varieties of this theology circulated among a wide range of divines, from antinomians like John Eaton to Church of England men like Lancelot Andrewes. Indeed, this theological range is often indexed by different uses of "disability." While some divines averred that humankind was "disabled to all" good by the first fatal breach,[74] for others, "the blow that sinne gave, made not an equall disabilitie to all actions."[75] The prevalence and depth of this "disability" could be shifted, but so could the location: It might be the heart, the eye, or even the "brain [that] is faulty."[76] In this sense, Calvinistic divines broadly agreed that disability was natural and universal, but they differed meaningfully on the specifics of these features. Variations in formulation could be fateful, for they adjusted the membership of the elect, altered the accessibility of assurance, and renegotiated the limits of salvation.

For a constellation of political and cultural reasons ranging from the rise of the new science to the ejection of dissenting ministers, this theology was decisively deposed in the latter half of the seventeenth century.[77] Whereas before the Restoration this distinctively stringent species of Calvinism had provided "the dominant mode of religious thought in England,"[78] by the

---

[69] Gataker, *Joy*, 130; Downame, *Covenant*, 30; Ussher, *Body*, 144.

[70] Westminster, *Humble*, 13; Savoy, *Declaration*, 13.   [71] Owen, *Principles*, 23.

[72] McRuer, *Crip Theory*, 2.   [73] For example, Fletcher, *Historie*, 23; Hallywell, *Sacred*, 31.

[74] Adams, *Happines*, I.371.   [75] Covell, *Just*, 37.   [76] Edwards, *Plague*, 8.

[77] For accounts of (and challenges to) this "decline": Cragg, *Reason*; Howe, "Decline"; MacKinnon, "Calvinism"; Rivers, *Reason*; Spurr, *Restoration*; Wallace, *Predestination*.

[78] Hill, *Milton*, 268.

Glorious Revolution it had been largely displaced by more voluntaristic, cov-enantal theologies that valued human effort and ability. Though Calvinism did not fall entirely into "obscurity and insignificance,"[79] the cultural sea change was substantial. Formerly endorsed tenets, such as predestinate reprobation, were renounced as inhumane or monstrous. Modes of legalistic moralism (tying salvation to good behavior), which had previously been considered un-Christian, were now regularly propagated as the essence or design of Christianity. Many divines continued to claim loyalty to the Westminster Confession, and some, such as Owen and Bunyan, maintained theologies that resisted the tide. But the hardest edges of Reformed theology, the tenets that defined *high* Calvinism, were undoubtedly softened; the inexorability of pre-destination was muted, the alterity of the reprobate modulated, and the extra-neity of justification qualified. In practice, the attendant shift "from grace to moralism"[80] entailed an emphasis on holiness and obedience, which were increasingly valued as a condition, or even *cause*, of justification (rather than its *effect*). This reversal helped prepare the way for Enlightenment philosophy and political theory by providing a rational and sensitive avatar for the natural-ization of sensibility and the hallowing of democratic values.

The "decline" of high Calvinism was a watershed moment not only in the history of religion but also that of disability, since the repudiation of this theology disseminated a normative, universal capability to humankind.[81] "All men are capable of Salvation," divines like Robert Barclay argued,[82] since humans possessed the faculties necessary for effective godliness: reason, of course, but also habit-formation and sensibility. For the anti-Calvinist divines who largely won the day, humanity was not – could not be – utterly and universally disabled. The most unflinching expressions of this perspective are found among moralistic and latitudinarian divines like Jeremy Taylor and Isaac Barrow, but assertions like those of Robert Ferguson were unremarkable by the turn of the century:

> all Men are made sufficiently and equally capable, both for *Moral* and *Political Government*, being abundantly furnished with whatsoever Faculties or Powers are indispensably needful, for knowing and loving God, understanding and obeying his Precepts, accepting and relying upon a Mediator, giving unreserv'd Credit to revealed Truths, embracing and trusting Promises; fearing and dreading Threatnings; and for performing all

---

[79] Cragg, *Reason*, 30. For revisionist approaches emphasizing the persistence of Calvinism: Goodwin, "Myth"; Hampton, *Anti-Arminians*; Wallace, *Shapers*.

[80] Cooper, *Fear*, 29.

[81] On this process, particularly as it concerns rationality: Harrison, *Bible*; Kroll et al. (eds.), *Philosophy*; Placher, *Domestication*; Rivers, *Reason*.

[82] Barclay, *Possibility*, 15.

the Relative and Social Duties; which are exacted of us, either towards Superiors, Equals, or those that are beneath us.[83]

Though this exaltation of "all Men" aligned with developments in medicine and physiology, the logic of this enabling was often axiomatically theological, as we will see with Baxter. God "gives ability, or else he would not require it; man is not condemned for that he has not afforded him, or is not capable of, for he gives to all men liberally."[84]

But what about the Fall? Much of the persistent antipathy to human nature was channeled into a discourse of bad habits, which served to acknowledge the impact of the Fall while opening the possibility for redress and self-regulation. Archbishop Tillotson, perhaps the most influential latitudinarian divine of his day, provides an exemplary expression of this enabling process. As he sees it, the faculties of judgment and deliberation that a man uses in business and politics are the same that pertain to "spiritual things," in which

> every Man hath the same Power radically, that is, he hath the Faculties of Understanding and Will; but these are obstructed and hinder'd in their exercise, and strongly byassed a contrary way by the Power of Evil Inclinations and Habits ... But then we are not to Understand this Impotency to be absolutely natural, but accidental; not to be in the first Frame and Constitution of our Souls, but to have hapned upon the depravation of Nature. It is not a want of natural Faculties, but the binding of them up and hindring their Operations to certain purposes.[85]

Endowing humans with such "power" at the root level decisively amended the impediments to postlapsarian morality, since "obstruct[ion]" and "byass" are far more remediable than complete "impotence" and "utter disability." As Tillotson suggests, the intention was not (as opponents charged) to glorify humans but rather to open up space for moral self-regulation. Foreclosing exemptions to responsibility was equally essential; Taylor asserts that nobody could "plead disability" when God had "enable[d] us" all to ameliorate ourselves.[86] Holdouts like Owen and Bunyan complained that so exalting human ability reduced salvation to mere "humane nature" – "what is common to all the men on Earth."[87] But that was partly the point, and they found themselves increasingly on the defensive, struggling to justify a worldview that seemed incompatible with the yearning for social order and pacific uniformity that prevailed amid the Restoration.

Though assertions of universal capability are the most visible feature of this soteriological enabling, an equally important part was regulating the language

[83] Ferguson, *View*, 100. [84] Whitehead, *Light*, 31. [85] Tillotson, *Repentance*, 310–311. [86] Taylor, *Symbolon*, 676. [87] Bunyan, *Defence*, 12.

of disability, including the term "disability" itself. Since the theology that anti-Calvinists repudiated was premised on a distinctive paradigm of "disability," the definition and application of the term was a significant battleground in this clash over justice and practice. The process of soteriological enabling, in other words, involved not simply imputing "natural faculties" and capabilities to "all men," but also qualifying, circumscribing, and regulating the meaning and use of "disability" in ways that laid the groundwork for its status as an exceptional, unnatural state. In many cases, narrowing the scope of such "disability" served the purpose; Taylor asserts, for instance, that "our nature is not wholly disabled."[88] Other divines, such as the moderate Presbyterian (and mathematician) John Wallis, questioned "what disability there is in the *Will* of Man since the fall more th[a]n in the confirmed Angels and Saints in Heaven? . . . I see not wherein this disability doth appear."[89] Since high Calvinist soteriology was often condemned for recklessly exempting subjects from moral responsibility, many reconfigurations focused on recasting effects and consequences. The Cambridge Platonist Benjamin Whichcote characteristically asserted that it was "not so much the *Disability* of Mens Nature; as *their Neglect* and *Abuse*" that made them sin.[90] Perhaps most important was how the existing definition of disability was directly disputed, as when the Presbyterian divine William Bates explained that we should not

> conceive of this Disability, as if Sinners had not deliberative and elective Faculties to consider and choose what is best: such a Disability would be an Argument for their Innocence and Justification: Neither as if Men had a Will to forsake Sin, and wanted Power; like a miserable Slave that sighs after Liberty, but is fasten'd by heavy Fetters: but the perverse Will keeps them in Bondage: *They serve divers Lusts and Pleasures*, and delight in their Fetters. 'Tis a voluntary culpable Impotence join'd with a strong Reluctancy to Grace.[91]

Bates illustrates how the desuetude of disability reflected a shift in foundational notions of culpability. An inability to "choose what is best" (formerly the fate of hapless reprobates) would actually absolve someone of spiritual responsibility, so this cannot be the basic state of humankind. The impulse to assign such responsibilizing agency was partly ideological and tropological; the denaturalization of "disability" reflected an unwillingness, related to England's burgeoning participation in the slave trade, to imagine impotence and slavery as the definition of (the English) man. The very possibility of claiming the promised "Kingdom in the *Indies*," as Baxter put it, required that Englishmen be

---

[88] Taylor, *Deus*, 46.   [89] Wallis, *Truth*, 55.   [90] Whichcote, *Sermons*, 155.
[91] Bates, *Sermons*, 292.

capacitated at the very outset. It was in the act of freely accepting or refusing to "shi[p] with Christ" that a more legitimate justice could be anchored.[92] By 1671, the once orthodox doctrine of man's "utter disability and perfect impotence" was increasingly considered a "false and dangerous opinio[n]," not only "contrary to Reason" but antithetical to good sense and stable society.[93] After all, what kind of society, not to mention economy, could be built by people who thought their moral behavior was outside their power?

4 Disputing Disability, Conditioning Salvation

Richard Baxter was on the front lines of this semantic conflict. His audacious redefinition of human capability helped to antiquate the logic of high Calvinism and legitimate a more apparently humane system of justice. Influenced by Reformed theology but brashly carving his own way, Baxter developed and propounded a theology of justification that was effectively conditional and hypothetically universal. He saw the characteristic doctrines of high Calvinism, especially absolute reprobation and unconditional justification, as inhumane, incoherent, and incompatible with a proper understanding of God, human nature, and justice.[94] Inspired by divines from Augustine to Ames, Baxter vehemently argued that salvation was available to all persons who properly "perform[ed] the conditions of the Gospel,"[95] foremost among which were active faith and sincere obedience. Such modes of personal righteousness, cultivated through practices like reading and meditation, were a necessary "condition" of the salvific covenant that applied to "all mankind."[96] This perspective was originally articulated in his first published work, *Aphorismes of Justification*, which drew intense controversy for its works-oriented soteriology. To be sure, from his debut until his death Baxter maintained a category of "elect" who were saved unconditionally by "special grace," and he reserved all "legal righteousness" to Christ.[97] Humans provided only the "evangelical righteousness" demanded by the covenant that Christ had meritoriously established. But the "strange proportions" of the *Aphorismes*

---

[92] Baxter, *Poor*, 29–30.   [93] Fowler, *Design*, 262; Tillotson, *Natural*, 172–173.
[94] Exactly where this soteriology situated Baxter on the landscape of Reformed theology remains a matter of debate. Baxter himself considered his theology a "middle way" between the poles that defined his age: Arminianism and antinomianism, legalism and libertinism, free will and predetermination. A common label for his theology is 'Amyraldian'; Baxter highly valued Amyraldus, but he claimed that he developed his doctrine of universal redemption "before he ever saw either *Amyraldus, Davenant,* or any writer (except Dr *Twiss*) for that way" (*Certain Disputations*, B3ʳ).
[95] Baxter, *Aphorismes*, 108.
[96] Baxter, *An Apology*, 124; *Aphorismes*, 92, 107–108; *Poor*, 54; *Right Method*, 190, 274, 453–454; *Saints*, 17; *Sermon of Judgement*, 183–189.
[97] Baxter, *Saints*, 402; *Christian Directory*, 324; L394.

("ten pages on the part God plays in our salvation; 325 pages on our own responsibility"[98]) lay the foundational shape of his oeuvre; even as he formally preserved God's absolute sovereignty, Baxter committed his attention and energy to the demands of personal righteousness. And with good reason; unlike the limited and indeterminate dynamics of special election, this conditional covenant entailed a law from which "no man on earth is excluded." "Shew where you are excluded if you can," he dared doubtful readers in his *Right Method for a Settled Peace of Conscience*.[99] He averred constantly and vehemently that the portion of "common grace" provided to every person could save them (if properly employed).[100] In practice, it was ultimately up to each individual whether or not they would be saved – an awesome and terrible responsibility.

The historical ramifications of this soteriological enabling, encoded as it was in his widely popular moral guidebooks, are far-reaching. Baxter proffered a persuasive paradigm of self-discipline and moral autonomy that made rehabilitation a universal and perpetual ideal. As he saw it, it would be absurd to submit to an inscrutable sovereignty that might (or might not) proffer grace arbitrarily; a system regulated by an appropriately standardized, legible law made far more sense. Under the "law of Grace" established by Christ, every person was given "the *use of certain duties* and *means* for their *Recovery*," a dispensation that reformed the moral landscape.[101] Since everyone was provided with the abilities they needed, there were none who were irrevocably or inherently disabled by nature. The condemned were only those who willfully refused or failed to satisfy these conditions.[102] Certainly, the Fall had engendered considerable backwardness and imperfection, and a large contingent of humankind *would* consequently suffer damnation. But *nobody*, Baxter was emphatic, was incapable of fulfilling this covenant.

This yoked commitment to "universal" inclusion and conditional salvation entailed a normative imputation of universal ability, one that arguably underpins the procedural ableism of liberal theory. For this theology to hold water, "all men" *must* necessarily "have a *natural power* or faculties, enabled to all that is *necessary to salvation*."[103] "God giveth men natural faculties," Baxter announced, and salvation hinged on their proper and effective use.[104] Though the Fall had bred bad habits and bad attitudes, Baxter was confident that all the "*natural Power* and *Liberty* which was essential to the Will, remaineth in it

---

[98] Cooper, "Calvinism," 331.   [99] Baxter, *Right Method*, 33–34; *Saints*, 137.

[100] Baxter, *Aphorismes*, 141–142; *End*, 176; *Universal*, 212, 279, 437.

[101] Baxter, *Catholick Theologie*, 45.

[102] Baxter, *Sermon of Judgement*, 156–157; *An Apology*, 123–127.

[103] Baxter, *Catholick Theologie*, 46.   [104] Baxter, *Right Method*, 25.

since the Fall."[105] He emphasized that this was not "free-will" in the established sense, but rather a "natural Liberty" oriented to rehabilitation; it was regulating and reforming our "vicious disposition[s]" that "every man" was equipped for.[106] This is an important distinction, for whereas a less constrained conception of freedom might have privileged different forms of embodiment (such as those attendant to "idiocy" or "melancholy"), Baxter proffered a power to return and remain within the bounds of "ordinary" capability. Though he could anatomize our "Natural faculties" with precision,[107] his assertions about human abilities emerge from an impulse to admonish and arouse rather than analyze. Thus while his vision of *natural power* included reason, anything necessary to standard salvation – most notably willpower – was within the natural power of man by definition.

There were, however, larger concerns than the individual conscience; membership in humanity was at stake in this reconfiguration, and Baxter aimed quite clearly to unite "all men" into a single "species." The hard boundary between elect and reprobate had traditionally bifurcated humanity irrevocably. Based on passages like 2 Peter 2:12, reprobates were "as natural brute beasts, made to be taken and destroyed." In most writing, reprobates were considered beastly or dead, such that they had no moral agency or value; "as they live so they dye, like very bruit beasts."[108] Baxter sought to dissolve this hard boundary between elect and reprobate, arguing that sin and grace do not "change our species" – "as if a *sinner* were not still a *man!*"[109] In this mode, Baxter was aiming not just at personal comfort but at political stability; his 1675 *Catholick Theologie* (i.e. inclusive theology), from which the above objection is drawn, promises to rebuff "incendiaries" and "dividers" with some "pacifying principles" about "Mans Power, Free-will, Justification, [and] Merits."[110] This layered personal and political imperative is behind his abiding endeavor to grant the same form of moral personhood to "all men," albeit through a normate that was unevenly applicable. His approach thus raises important questions about the value and ramifications – conceptual, ethical, and political – of *reducing* difference; doing so allowed Baxter to incorporate a significant degree of diversity, but equally prevented him from abiding alterity. He would have abjured neomaterialist and "dismodernist" paradigms of disability,[111] filiated as they are with materialism and antinomianism. Though Baxter was no stranger to natural philosophy, the

---

[105] Baxter, *End*, 173.
[106] Baxter, *Gildas*, 475–476; *An Apology*, 124–125. Also, *Right Method*, 251–252; *Sermon of Judgement*, 141–142.
[107] Baxter, *Christian Directory*, 587. Also, *Aphorismes*, 250–255. [108] Jerome, *Haughty*, 102.
[109] Baxter, *Catholick Theologie*, 40; *End*, 176–177; *Christian Directory*, 324.
[110] Baxter, *Catholick Theologie*, frontispiece. [111] Davis, *Dismodernism*, 30.

logic of this universal enabling was primarily theological, appealing to the perfect aptitude of divine government: Whatever God has commanded, humans must logically be equipped to perform. God works by fit means, treating "man" as "a *living free self-determining* Agent" capable of comprehension, contracts, and consent.[112] As he put it succinctly in 1670, "it is fit that the Government of God be suited to the *nature* of the *reasonable* subject."[113] Baxter was enthralled by the logical exactness of this divine government,[114] and he demonstrates how an ideology of ability could be rooted not in an anatomized body (which was indeed imperfect and variable) but in the legal subject it betokened, which was perfectly fit for the role it occupied in the perfectly designed "law of grace."

In building a system of universal redemption so firmly on an able-bodied normate, Baxter encountered a germinal expression of the problem of justice identified by theorists like Nussbaum and Hirschmann:[115] Individuals with impairments were systemically disadvantaged or even excluded in ways that were incongruous with the promise of universal inclusion. The theodical and ecclesiological issues attendant on disability were not new, but redefining soteriology and justice put Baxter in a uniquely fraught position. He ambitiously advertised universal access, but he was averse to many of the most established responses to the problems presented by disability. Compare, for instance, how John Milton accounts for the apparent exclusion of the impotent (arguably blind) speaker in Sonnet 19. He initially agonizes over his "useless" talent, worrying that God will admonish him for failing to labor as profitably as others; he thinks that God will hold him to an unvarying standard that disregards his disability. But this rigidly transactional logic is displaced by inscrutable gratuity. The absolute sovereignty of God, who "doth not need / Either man's work or his own gifts," renders human distinctions between mobility and immobility, ability and disability, deserving and undeserving effectively inconsequential.[116]

Whereas Milton invokes this problem to impugn an ideology of ability (i.e. works-righteousness), Baxter characteristically responds to disability by reinforcing and refining the purview of human capability. Indeed, Baxter uses this same parable (Matthew 25:14–30) to remind faltering readers that they invariably have alternative talents: "if you have not one, you have another," he maintains.[117] Rather than repudiate standardized measurement, Baxter thus reinforces its reach and legitimacy. The angelic intercessor he envisions offers consolation with conditions, announcing that "if thou wilt have Christ and Life in him, thou shalt."[118] There is a world of difference, both for theology and

---

[112] Baxter, *Life of Faith*, 226.   [113] Ibid., 9.   [114] Burton, *Hallowing*; Packer, *Quest*.
[115] Nussbaum, *Frontiers*; Hirschmann, "Freedom and (Dis)Ability"; "Disability Rights."
[116] Milton, "Sonnet," ln.4, 9–10.   [117] Baxter, *Right Method*, 336.   [118] Ibid., 46.

disability, between the paradigms these responses represent: Conditioning salvation imposes a set of demands that could be unfair or inaccessible. For personal and political reasons we will explore, Baxter was deeply invested in an ideology of ability that would disincentivize passivity – "stand[ing] and wait[ing]"[119] for supernatural intervention. As he saw it, a soteriology built around capability and action was evidently better suited to a species possessing natural faculties. In his resolutely pragmatic *Life of Faith*, which built upon a sermon he preached before Charles II at the Restoration, Baxter sought to excite indolent readers to godliness with an instructive contrast: Imagine if, on the one hand, "there were one Law made, that men should *lie* or *stand still* all the day, with their eyes shut, and their ears stopped, and their mouths closed, and that they should not *stir*, nor *see*, nor *hear*, nor *taste*," while, on the other hand, "another Law that man should *use* their *eyes*, and *ears*, and *limbs*, &c." "Which of these" laws, he asked readers rhetorically, "were more suitable to *humanity*, and more easie for a sound man to obey (though the first might best suit with the *lame*, and *blind*, and *sick*)."[120]

The (parenthetical) persistence of disability here, however, is characteristic. Baxter acknowledged impairment as a common feature of the species he imagined, but its implications had to be marginalized, so that it did not demand or legitimate an alternative soteriology. He was markedly sensitive to the realities of impairment, and he was hardly aiming to exclude persons with disabilities. Not only would this contradict many biblical passages, but it would also remap absolute reprobation onto the body – predestined damnation for disabled persons. He readily acknowledged, if only to comfort doubtful readers, that God would never hang "our salvation upon the strength of our Memories, the Readiness of our Tongues, or measure of the like Gifts," since this would yield a patently unfair law: Only those with "sound Complexions, and healthfull and youthfull bodies" would be saved, while any that "are sickly, aged, weak, children, and most women" would be damned.[121] On the contrary, the covenant of grace was supposed to be practicable; the "labour" required of each person was not, as Baxter saw it, prohibitively onerous. A "peppercorn rent"[122] of sincere commitment and diligent effort was seemingly within the means of even the most infirm of laborers.

But however generous or easy, such "conditions" necessarily disadvantaged persons with disabilities, since their "performance" might be impaired, unrecognized, or even impossible within the established parameters. After all, the demands of "rationall diligence"[123] and energetic labor favor specific

---

[119] Milton, "Sonnet," ln.14.   [120] Baxter, *Life of Faith*, 232–233.
[121] Baxter, *Right Method*, 451.   [122] See Boersma, *Pepper Corn*.
[123] Baxter, *True Christianity*, 35.

configurations of faculties. Baxter grappled with this problem, but his attempts to redress or resolve it (if that was finally possible) were inhibited by his anxieties about competing soteriologies; hemmed in on every side by Papists and antinomians, backsliders and Baptists, Baxter rarely felt that he could entertain the implications of the exceptions disability entailed. He certainly could not allow everyone to pursue their own unique path to heaven, for this would lead many hapless souls to "delusion and perdition." He feared the "free" salvation proffered by varieties of Calvinism, and he worried equally about its counterpart among the common people, so many of whom thought they were saved simply "because they believe."[124] Merely *feeling* like you were saved or *wanting* to be saved was not enough (and even *trying* was often insufficient). In the face of impairment, any impulse to relax or adjust the conditions of salvation was counteracted by this imperative to invalidate other soteriological systems.

In his perpetual campaign against such fatal falsehoods, Baxter was driven to amplify the laboriousness, "*skill* and *diligence*" that salvation involved,[125] a tendency that engendered ableist dynamics. Thus what he broadly expressed as an easy condition – merely "accepting" or believing in Christ[126] – became, in practice, constrained by standardized duties of obedience, manifestations of willingness, and performances of sincerity. There was, in a word, "a great deal more th[a]n believing" necessary.[127] Metaphors are frequently a register for underlying norms of capability, and Baxter's often betray how exclusionary this system could be. Salvation, he said, was like a cutthroat race or a weightlifting competition: The slowest and weakest should never have bothered.[128] Though he was not as profit-minded as Weber suggests, he does frequently invoke the brutal logic of the market to denigrate the "multitudes" of sinners who, like "idle beggars," refused to "labour painfully" for their salvation. Citing passages like 2 Thessalonians 3:10, Baxter often reminded his readers that "if any would not work, neither should he eat,"[129] an arrangement in which people incapable of so working were always precarious or treacherous anomalies.

Though Baxter's opponents and critics were inveighing against Popery and Arminianism rather than paternalism and neoliberalism, they saw how his exaltation of human ability and agency raised problems of justice. In ways that recall Berlant's critique of "cruel optimism,"[130] opponents argued that the liberty Baxter offered was only specious. John Owen, his most eminent nemesis among Calvinist divines, contended that conditional salvation was "promis[ing] to give a 1000^l, to a blind man upon condition that he will open his eyes and

---

[124] Baxter, *Baxters Apology*, 8. Also, *Life of Faith*, 15–16.
[125] Baxter, *Christian Directory*, 72.   [126] Baxter, *Saints*, 158.
[127] Baxter, *True Christianity*, 131. Also, *Baxters Apology*, 62–63, 82.   [128] Baxter, *Saints*, 358.
[129] Ibid., 364.   [130] Berlant, *Optimism*.

see"[131]; to "open a doore for him to come out of Prison, who is blinde and lame" was to "deride his misery" rather than "procure him liberty."[132] Many targeted denunciations of "Baxterianism" were satirical and parodic, and these captured even more pointedly the connections between conceptual inconsistency and systemic injustice. In 1659, the anti-Calvinist Laurence Womock dramatically parodied "Master *Baxters* Administrations" to the "non-elect." "Sir, you are in a very sad condition," the mock-Baxter explains,

> and nothing is to be expected but sudden death, unless you will submit to our directions and Prescriptions to prevent it. I see, God be thanked, you have all your naturall faculties, your mouth and your stomack, and here I offer you an excellent Physitian, and I intreat you heartily to be advised by him; he will give you Physick shall be wholesome and work very gently, it may stirre the humour a little, but there is no danger of working too much, for indeed 'tis uneffectuall.[133]

Womock captures not only Baxter's distinctive regard for "naturall faculties" (though mouth and stomach are perhaps less dignified than reason and will), but also the cruelty that attends his offers of salvation – a dying man given ineffective medicines. While some of these arguments invoked disability metaphorically, others pointed out the practical inequities of privileging performance in a physiologically heterogeneous world. Divines like William Prynne and William Eyre argued, for instance, that there could be "no conditions required of us" because "Ideots" and "Lunatiques" would be cruelly condemned by default.[134]

As the gravity of this systemic snag depended on the prevalence of disability, Baxter carefully policed the definition and application of the term, to ensure that it would not represent a significant exception to the universal reach of capability. As theorists like Campbell and Simplican have demonstrated, a theory of justice premised on ability, as Baxter's was, requires that disability be constantly "unthought" or "disavow[ed]."[135] The more profoundly disability represents an exception, the less legitimate and applicable systemic assumptions about capability become. Driven by the imperative to put off this problem, Baxter's gatekeeping of disability functioned not only to impugn high Calvinist soteriology, but also to address a tension at the heart of his own: God would never demand "impossibilities,"[136] and yet the performance universally required by the covenant of grace was not universally accessible. In narrowing the use of the term "disability," Baxter was served well by his notorious knack

---

[131] Owen, *Salus*, 109–110, 309.   [132] Ibid., 316.   [133] Womock, *Arcana*, 194–195.
[134] Prynne, *Church*, 96; Eyre, *Vindiciae*, 192–193.
[135] Campbell, "Legislating," 109; Simplican, *Capacity Contract*, 71–92.
[136] Baxter, *Christian Directory*, 281; *Universal*, 214–217.

for semantic sifting (one critic joked that he could "distinguish and distinguish till he had distinguish'd all into nothing"[137]). He divided and subdivided disability into dust, differentiating between "disability *Antecedent* to the Law, and Consequent"; between "Mediate and Immediate" disability; between "Impossibles as such, and as *Things Hated* or *Nilled*," and "between *Primary* and *Secondary* Moral acts."[138] What people typically called "disability," Baxter suggested, was actually "*Moral Vicious Impotency*" – bad habits or personal failings for which they would be rightly punished.[139] "Thats not fitly called disability,"[140] he responded to those who used the term incorrectly. And it was many who did so, since Baxter would have "disability" play little to no role in the lexicon of salvation and justice.

Some of these skirmishes over the definition involved theological intricacies (about the *ordo salutis*, *potentia*, and materialism) that are too complex to unpack here, but Baxter was a practical theologian and even at his most abstruse he had an abiding aim: to assert the unlimited reach of "natural" faculties. He was genuinely concerned about the practical side of this issue; to call bad habits or personal failings disability was a misnomer of fatal consequence. If secularism is defined substantially by practices of "differentiation,"[141] then such semantic differentiation was arguably part of this process, for it made possible a morally autonomous individual by partitioning off an entire mode of spiritual experience. But Scripture was filled with examples of disability, wasn't it? These scenes often marked the needfulness of gratuitous dispensation – of salvation proffered *without* conditions. But Baxter was generally unconvinced; he collated nearly thirty instances and concluded confidently that "you will not say it is *natural* and *utter disability* that is here spoken of."[142] In a profound sense, "disability" no longer existed in the system Baxter envisioned: To be human was to have natural ability, so there was no position from which such capability could be renounced.[143]

Though important to the lexicographic history of the topic, this differentiation of "disability" was more than rarefied theological wrangling. The imperative to circumscribe and capacitate shaped Baxter's response to disability at the

---

[137] [Young], *Anti-Baxterianæ*, 86.   [138] Baxter, *Catholick Theologie*, 39.   [139] Ibid.

[140] Baxter, *Baxters Apology*, 29.

[141] Bruce, "Differentiation"; Casanova, *Public*, 11–25; Luhmann, *Differentiation*; Parsons, *Societies*.

[142] Baxter, *Catholick Theologie*, 45.

[143] Baxter did have a role for "disability" in his soteriology, one that relegated the phenomenon to practical irrelevance; postlapsarian mankind was "disabled" in relation to the "first covenant," which required obedience to the original law. This covenant, however, was supplemented by the "new" covenant established by Christ that offered conditions "in reference to the strength which God will bestow, are far more facile" (*Aphorismes*, 77). In this sense, "disability" existed historically but not presently; it was an obsolete category.

personal level, yielding a normative ableism that could be remarkably unforgiving. "Do not *say I cannot*": This was the essence of his advice to virtually all readers who appealed to disability.[144] Though Baxter admitted the physiological reality of impairment, he could not allow disability to be "claimed" in the sense elucidated by theorists like Simi Linton as a "vantage point of the atypical."[145] To do so would scuttle all attempts at standardization and discipline, permitting (as he saw it) a theologically-countenanced indolence and licentiousness. The relentless capacitation he pursued was meant to be encouraging, designed to reassure readers of their potential and agency, and his correspondence confirms that it often was; Baxter was undeniably good at pushing people to push themselves. But precisely because this approach was rooted in normative capability, appeals to "disability" had to be met with an intransigence which exposed the hard edge of his soteriology. To invoke impotence or incapacity, he typically suggested, was little more than an evasion of responsibility, a "frivolous excuse" or "vain Cavi[l]."[146] He admonished those who complained of "wandring thoughts" and "bad memory,"[147] and he almost never doubted that readers were largely at fault for their failings. "Pretend not to disability for carnal unwillingness and laziness," he warned, for doing so would only aggravate culpability: "your *disabily* [sic] is your very *unwillingness* it self, which excuseth not your sin, but maketh it the greater."[148] Since he defined human identity on the grounds of capability, those who fell short in the conditional schema he envisioned necessarily did so by virtue of dilatoriness rather than disability. When he imagined readers appealing to such a category to question the demands of the conditional covenant, he answered them trenchantly: "You were not *Able*, because you were not *Willing*."[149] The sometimes jarring dissonance between the systemic motives of this soteriology – divine love and everyday holiness – and the response to disability alerts us to a strain that goes far deeper than semantics.

This categorical aversion to disability is perhaps most apparent in his invocations of impairment, which serve quite transparently to consolidate or expand the purview of ability. Whereas Calvinist writers often looked to conditions such as "lameness" or blindness as an opportunity to impugn human power, Baxter does so typically as a means of reminding readers that they are irreducibly capable. In his 1662 *The Mischiefs of Self-Ignorance*, a set of sermons written to enjoin his readers (and former parishioners) to saving self-knowledge, Baxter acknowledges that "as to *Ability*," there may be individuals

---

144 Baxter, "Cure of Melancholy," 292.   145 Linton, *Claiming*, 5.
146 Baxter, *Dying Thoughts*, 325; *Two Treatises*, 58.   147 Baxter, *Right Method*, 305.
148 Baxter, *Call*, 231. Also, *Sermon of Judgement*, 143.
149 Baxter, *Sermon of Judgement*, 130. Also, *Saints*, 292; *Right Method*, 309.

with "*Impediments* of some *Natural disability,* or *excessive bashfulness, Melancholy* or the *like disease.*" But these figures instantly drop out of the picture, since Baxter imagines the reader as self-evidently among those "that are of as good *naturall parts* and *free elocution* as other men."[150] In his writing on a "calling" the same dynamics emerge, Baxter conceding the pathological exception so he can confirm the rule: "disability indeed is an unresistable impediment," but "every one that is able, must be *statedly,* and *ordinarily* imployed in such work, as is serviceable to God, and the common Good."[151] With such maneuvers the reader is invited, or often shamed, into admitting that while such exceptions might theoretically exist somewhere, they are systemically and personally irrelevant: It can never be *you* who "hath a good excuse."[152] Indeed, in most cases this disability is purely hypothetical, and Baxter is rarely able to make it through a full sentence of even speculative concession: "if you were *willing* to be the Servant of Christ, and yet were not able either because he would not accept you, or because of a want of natural Faculties, or because of some other natural Difficulty which the *willingest* Mind could not overcome, this were some Excuse: But to be habitually wilful in refusing Grace, is worse than to be meerly actually unwilling."[153] We might object that Baxter is writing for a mass audience, so he naturally imagines his readers as ordinary rather than extraordinary. But this makes such moments no less remarkable; Baxter constructs his reader, quite compellingly, as presumptively able-bodied – capable of impregnable self-regulation, self-knowledge, and rehabilitation. The ascendancy of liberal personhood has made this authorial stance seem undeniably natural: Of course the 'common reader' is not disabled. But the backlash Baxter received for exalting capability and self-determination reminds us how historically contingent this imagined reader is, emerging as it did in the face of a tradition that regularly figured the ordinary reader as fallen, infirm, and impotent.

Baxter contributed significantly to the streams of tolerance and liberalism that we inherited from the Enlightenment, so it is worth considering the origins of his aversion to disability. This bias manifests most appealingly in his visions of social unity, which coalesced around his able-bodied normate. By treating the human as a capable creature, the rationalistic "law of grace" made it possible to form "one universal Church" around shared capacities.[154] While his theology can be traced back to specific influences such as Scotus, Amyraldus, and Davenant, doing so does not reveal *why* Baxter was so powerfully drawn down this particular path to social harmony – rather than, say, to the unfettered "unitie, peace, and love"

---

[150] Baxter, *Mischiefs,* 177.   [151] Baxter, *Christian Directory,* 133.
[152] Baxter, *Directions and Perswasions,* 91.   [153] Baxter, *Two Treatises,* 59.   [154] L359.

offered by a radical Calvinist like John Saltmarsh.[155] Why not foreground the "extraordinary workings" of salvation,[156] as many divines did in the face of disability? Why not explain to Christians with disabilities who were faced with apparent "impossibilities" that God imputed grace freely and unconditionally, rather than demand that they push themselves, perhaps to death?

For all his attachment to peace and harmony, Baxter was spurred most sharply by a fierce crusade against a monster that stalked the land and preyed upon its people: antinomianism. A controversial form of Calvinism that offered its own logic of equality and justice, antinomianism so elevated the gratuitousness of grace that the law (*nomos*) was rendered irrelevant; as antinomians like Saltmarsh and Eaton saw it, obeying moral laws was entirely unnecessary (though righteousness could be an *effect* of justification). Baxter believed that such a worldview, with its "free grace" and euphoric fellowship, could lead only to personal licentiousness and social anarchy,[157] partly because the fear of punishment was "the groundwork of all Laws and Government," both earthly and divine.[158] His consequent animosity toward antinomianism (and those that seemed to countenance it) would be hard to overstate. He confessed that his "detestation of these destructive Antinomian Principles" sometimes made him "run out further against them th[a]n [he] intended."[159] But he often couldn't help himself. Invocations of monstrosity gather around the topic in his writing, as when he flaunted the stillbirths – "the two Monsters in *New England*" – of Anne Hutchinson and Mary Dyer to traduce their "monstrous" antinomian beliefs.[160]

The stridency of Baxter's ableism on this topic is no coincidence; abhorrence of antinomianism colored, and perhaps even tainted, his theology, particularly as it pertained to weakness and disability. He is constantly anticipating imagined antinomian objections and stratagems, most of all when he is providing comfort and guidance to readers. Since it offered a less laborious schema of salvation, antinomianism appealed, Baxter believed, to weak and ill individuals. The "methods for comforting troubled souls" thus became an important arena in a nasty ground war with these "slanderous Antinomians."[161] To discredit the opiate-laced palliatives they peddled,[162] Baxter had to amplify rather than mollify his emphasis on "gospel obedience." The constant threat of antinomianism, in other words, dissuaded Baxter from permitting extralegal processes of salvation – special exemptions, exceptions, and dispensations.[163] Rather than

---

[155] Saltmarsh, *Reasons*.   [156] Gataker, *Joy*, 245.
[157] Baxter, *Life of Faith*, 298; *Right Method*, 215.   [158] Baxter, *Right Method*, 135.
[159] Ibid., 218.   [160] Baxter, *Saints*, a1ʳ, 232.   [161] Baxter, *Right Method*, b1ʳ, 415.
[162] Ibid., b1ʳ.
[163] Baxter did not entirely deny that such extralegal processes were within God's power, but he was reluctant to endorse them; "special Providences" were "not to be as common as the General, nor to subvert Gods ordinary established Course of Government" (ibid., 26).

illustrate the needfulness of systemic adjustment or reform, the extraordinary circumstances of disability thus occasioned an intensified emphasis on "Gods ordinary way of giving Grace."[164] Though his anxieties about antinomianism fluctuated with the times, his theology was originally honed against it, such that it long shaped his attitude toward disability. As Samuel Rutherford pointed out, antinomianism promised the "lame" that they could be saved *without* rehabilitation – a logic that would "put all Divines to Schoole againe" to reconsider the binaries of sight and blindness, health and illness.[165] Baxter was not interested in going back to school, not least because his lessons on antinomianism had been so hard earned.

Contextualizing his hostility toward antinomianism illustrates how the moral panic evoked by disability is rooted deeply in sociolegal anxieties not just about justice and laws, but about the systemic coherence of the legal subject. Behind Baxter's flailing opposition to antinomianism was no small degree of personal trauma. His harrowing experience of the Civil War, during which he served as chaplain for a parliamentary regiment, forged an indelible association between the lawlessness that antinomianism ostensibly authorized and the "heart-piercing spectacles" he witnessed: brethren wounded, friends slain, battlefields strewn with the carcasses of his countrymen.[166] As Tim Cooper has documented, antinomianism, knitted as it was to Baxter's experience of the Civil War, became a "manifestation of his inner fears" about "a world turned upside down, and inside out."[167] Theorists have variously suggested that "disability is the unorthodox made flesh,"[168] and for Baxter such unorthodoxy slid seamlessly from the personal to the theological to the political. Disability underscored the problems with a uniform "law of grace," and thus it threatened the juridical uniformity that undergirded theological and social order. This trajectory is apparent in a work like his *Call to the Unconverted*, in which he illustrates his claim that "your *disabily* [sic] is your very *unwillingness* it self" with a set of sensationalized thought experiments that dramatize the juridical danger of the category: Imagine, if you will, that "you have an enemy so malicious, that he falls upon you, and beats you every time he meets you, and takes away the lives of your children, will you excuse him because he saith *I have not free will, it is my nature; I cannot choose unless God give me grace?*" Would you, he asked readers, absolve a thieving servant or an unfaithful wife on such grounds?[169] Would a judge or jury exonerate a murderer or thief because he said he could not help himself?[170] Because he framed divine justice in such human terms, disability could never be granted soteriological significance,

---

[164] Ibid., 136.   [165] Rutherford, *Survey*, II.110–111.   [166] Baxter, *Saints*, 122–123.
[167] Cooper, *Fear*, 7.   [168] Garland-Thomson, *Extraordinary*, 24.   [169] Baxter, *Call*, 231–233.
[170] Baxter, *Sermon of Judgement*, 146.

since to do so would hamstring judicial process: "might not every Thief and Murderer that is hanged at the Assize give such an answer ... *I have not free-will; I cannot change my own heart: what can I do without Gods grace?*"[171] Disability Studies scholars have noted how much ableism is rooted in the law,[172] but Baxter illustrates how this connection might go deeper than usually thought – to the theological and metaphysical connections between law, justice, and moral personhood.

Today the juridical complexities of disability are significantly governed by medical authority, but I have deferred discussing medicine so that it could be situated as a consequence rather than a cause of broader theological attitudes toward disability in seventeenth-century England. Though the 'medicalization' of disability is often traced to the eighteenth and nineteenth centuries, Allison Hobgood and David Wood have recently posited a "protomedical" model taking form in seventeenth-century writing, one that combined "moralizing fears" with "scientifically driven rationalizations."[173] Baxter illustrates how the logic of this model might work, but also how it differed importantly from strictly 'medical' thinking. The doctrine of personal responsibility is girded by medical tropes, but Baxter's motives are ultimately religious – the saving of souls rather than just bodies. Yet, these theological motivations do entail medically oriented consequences; in making "every man" potentially salvageable, Baxter natural-ized the rehabilitative rationale that defines modern medicine.

As Baxter figures it, attitudes toward medical care were inseparable from the soteriologico-politico conflicts of his age. Disdaining medical authority, Baxter argued, was analogous to the "foolish reasoning" of antinomians. To "question whether we may Believe and Obey for our own Salvation" was effectively the same as "question[ing] whether we may go to the Physician, and follow his advice for Health and Life."[174] As such, doubts about the legitimacy of medical intervention had to be stamped out. Thus while Baxter does not exalt medicine for its own sake, he nonetheless frames submission to its rules as a structural corollary of conditional salvation. But this is not a unidirectional analogy: A proper understanding of conditional salvation actually entails accepting medical reasoning in earthly life. In his *Christian Directory*, a detailed reference guide providing precepts on every-thing from sports to slavery, Baxter explains that the promise of life, both earthly and everlasting, encompassed *all* the means God had provided, medi-cine prominently among them:

---

[171] Baxter, *Call*, 233.

[172] Campbell, *Contours*, 30–44, 130–159; Steele and Thomas (eds.), *Griffith*.

[173] Hobgood and Wood, "Literature," 35.   [174] Baxter, *Right Method*, a7ᵛ–a8ʳ.

As God hath appointed no man to salvation simply without respect to the *means* of salvation; so God hath appointed no man to *live*, but by the *means* of life. His Decree is not (*Such a man shall be saved*) or (*Such a man shall live so long*) only. But this is his Decree, [*Such a man shall be saved, in the way of faith and holiness, and in the diligent use of means*] and [*Such a man shall live so long, by the use of those means which I have fitted for the preservation of his life:*] So that as he that *liveth a holy life* may be sure he is chosen to salvation (if he persevere) and he that is ungodly may be sure that he is in the way to Hell; so he that neglecteth the *means* of his health and life, doth shew that it is unlike that God hath appointed him to live: and he that useth the best means is liker to recover.[175]

Baxter demonstrates how foundational attitudes to medicine could be rooted in a specific soteriology; while a rigidly predestinarian worldview would make medical treatment pointless, the conditional framework that Baxter helped propagate entailed a weighty responsibility to care for one's health. Without actually discussing the complexities of medicine or doctors, Baxter formulates a logic that is foundational to the medical model: Resisting or neglecting medical treatment is immoral, since the norms of moral responsibility are reciprocally supported – "joyned together" with – practices of self-regulation. In effect, to disdain the "means" of salvation is to deliberately adopt a passivity that must always be radically exceptional.

Yet, while Baxter directed his readers to heed "the ablest Physicions" and castigated those who deigned to trust in God passively, he did not intend that one should simply submit unthinkingly to doctors;[176] it was the rehabilitative logic of medicine, not specific practitioners, to which subjection was enjoined. A responsible and effective Christian life, in fact, required a substantial degree of independent medical expertise and self-treatment. Baxter regularly compared the acquisition of theologically "right knowledge" to medical training. A good Christian had to understand "not only the *Materialls* of an apothecaries shop, but also the *medicinall use* of the simples & compositions" (a mode of knowledge he ascribes to Robert Boyle).[177] The slippage between metaphor and materiality multiplies the responsibilities of the individual, for people should take advice, and physic, and advice on physic, and physic for advice. Baxter often characterized his spiritual directions as medical prescriptions, and in some cases they included actual prescriptions, as in his "Cure of Melancholy and Overmuch-Sorrow by Faith and Physick" which concludes with a series of affordable home remedies.[178] As this approach suggests, self-medication was an important part of self-regulation, not merely an extension but perhaps its

---

[175] Baxter, *Christian Directory*, 653.   [176] Ibid., 653.   [177] L720.
[178] Baxter, "Cure of Melancholy," 299–302.

essence. The fallibility of doctors meant that individuals had to be doctors themselves. Baxter thus subordinated mere "physick" to medically regulated regimes of self-care involving dietary discipline (including "diet drink[s]"), purging regimes (of senna and turpentine), physical exercise (daily), and customized self-medication.[179] In the saving of the body as of the soul, medical advice was important, but it was the individual who ultimately bore the responsibility for their treatment and prognosis.

Baxter himself figured as the paragon of this soteriologico-medical system, his fitful physiology – and his discursive mastery of it – giving the defining shape to his life and theology.[180] Respiratory difficulties, effusive nosebleeds, digestive disorders, painful inflammations, excoriated fingertips, swollen legs, debilitating foot pain, stubborn cataracts: The ailments that Baxter suffered were so numerous and severe that, for years at a time, he "scarce had a whole day free from some dolor," "scarce … a waking hour free from pain."[181] At one point he was seeing thirty-six physicians, though they were often of little help. His mobility was frequently impaired, as was his concentration, "the weakeness of [his] body" limiting him to "study but 2 or 3 hours in a day."[182]

Baxter's constant attention to the temporality of his experience evokes the accounts of "crip time" developed by theorists like Petra Kuppers and Alison Kafer, which elucidate the "challenge to normative and normalizing expectations of pace and scheduling."[183] Baxter discusses his health problems regularly throughout his prefaces and postscripts (so often that opponents mocked him for it), but the most detailed account is found in *Reliquiae Baxterianae*, his posthumous 800-page biography. There he describes how his typical day at Kidderminster was arranged around the demands of his body: "I could not bear (through the weakness of my Stomach)," he explains,

> to rise before Seven a Clock in the Morning, and afterwards not till much later; and some Infirmities I laboured under, made it above an hour before I could be drest. An hour I must of necessity have to walk before Dinner, and another before supper; and after Supper I can seldom Study: all which, besides times of Family Duties, and Prayer, and Eating, &c. leaveth me but little time to study; which hath been the greatest external Personal Affliction of all my Life.[184]

---

[179] Ibid., 299; *Gildas*, 391–392.
[180] Though the relationship between "illness" and "disability" has been a matter of debate (Wendell, "Unhealthy"), theorists have been increasingly inclined to treat "disability as a site of questions rather than firm definitions" (Kafer, *Feminist*, 11), such that it now often includes a wide range of phenomena, including neuroatypicality, chronic illness, mood disorders, temporary impairments, "invisible" disabilities, addiction, etc.
[181] Baxter, *Saints*, 126, A3ʳ. For the best account of his illness: Cooper, "Physicians."
[182] Baxter, *Reliquiae*, I.10; L18.   [183] Kafer, *Feminist*, 27; Kuppers, "Crip Time."
[184] Baxter, *Reliquiae*, I.84.

Baxter often describes this temporal discordance as an "affliction," but this is more self-consciously constructive than it might appear. "Affliction" was, after all, a salutary source of mortification in Christian thought, and Baxter contended that his early and lifelong proximity to death had furnished him with a unique perspective and power. The emotional intensity generated by this period recalls the "incredible wakefulness" attendant to illness described by Mel Chen, and Baxter similarly sought to recover or channel this energy during times of recovery. "I am confounded," he confessed, "to think what difference there is between my sickness apprehensions, and my Pulpit and discoursing apprehensions."[185] Yet he had no doubt that his "sickness apprehensions" had given him a heightened sense of temporality, illness having not only "taught [him] highly to esteem [his] Time," but also furnished an alternative form of expertise. Considering that he lacked the official university training boasted by many divines, his education in the "School of Affliction" was an invaluable source of authority, one that was as naturally systematic as a traditional curriculum: "weakness & paine helpt me to study how to die; & that set me on studying how to live, & that set me on studying the doctrine from which I must fetch my motives & Comforts, & beginning with Necessaryes I proceed to the Lesser integralls by degrees, & now am going to see that which I have lived & studied for."[186]

The discursive power Baxter achieved over his disability is remarkable, but it presents some methodological and ethical perplexities, since he often used this power to consolidate his ideology of ability, most notably by figuring his illness as a paradigmatic story of personal culpability. Though he proffered a range of explanations for his chronic infirmities, he returned to a gastrointestinal etiology: In his youth he "was much addicted to the excessive gluttonous eating of Apples and Pears," a habit that probably "laid the foundation of that *Imbecillity* and Flatulency of my Stomach, which caused the Bodily Calamities of my Life."[187] This origin story clearly attaches personal culpability to disability, a connection Baxter girds with profound theological import when he transforms it from a personal experience into a moral lesson:

> Sinful Souls! Look back upon the folly, which was the cause of all thy pains. As *Adam* and *Eves* sin brought suffering into the world, upon our natures, so my own sin is the cause of my own particular suffering. A sinful pleasing of my appetite with raw Apples, Pears, and Plums, when I was young, did lay the foundation of all my uncurable Diseases: And my many offences since deserved God's Chastisements.[188]

[185] Chen, *Animacies*, 1; Baxter, *Gildas*, 370–371.   [186] Baxter, *Dying Thoughts*, 222; L1065.
[187] Baxter, *Reliquiae*, I.2.   [188] Baxter, *Obedient*, 29–30.

Baxter acknowledged this peculiar affinity with Augustine, who had confessed to stealing pears from a neighboring orchard with his adolescent cronies. But a series of adjustments tighten the personal responsibility enjoined by the story. Whereas in the *Confessions* this transgression is primarily symbolic, serving to illustrate the perversity of human nature, in Baxter's version cause and effect are rooted more directly in personal physiology. Presumably, the "particular" pains of each person are legibly traceable to a particular bad habit, such as overeating, sleeping in, or tippling.

This passage illustrates how the adverse legacy of Christianity, which is often said to stigmatize disability, is more convoluted and contingent than it seems. Historians of disability have often argued that the 'moral model' rooted in Christianity ascribes disability to sin. There is some truth to this, but the significance of this connection – how substantially it stigmatizes and patholo-gizes – crucially depends on the underlying hamartiology. If sin is natural and universal, as it was within the parameters of Calvinist orthodoxy, the deficiency that disability symbolizes might be that of the human condition. A disability might indeed be a punishment for sin, but for the same sin – original, inherent, natural – for which everyone has such guilt. Conversely, personalizing sin by making it a matter of individual morality rather than essential nature assigns to disability a distinctively depreciatory inflection, as it does in Baxter's figuration. It is in this framework that illness and impairment can indeed be read as a personal punishment.

Shifting from connate to physiological causation takes quite a leap, of course, and Baxter must reorient many of the established hamartiological conventions to take it. The act of collectively "look[ing] back" to the Fall is invoked, but this original transgression switches from etiology to analogy ("as ... so"): Each body is a microcosmic world of its own, running in parallel (rather than lineage) with the Fall. In this system, every individual has their own distinctive original sin. In other words, personal sin is not genetically inherited but physiologically precipitated. But why, at the *individual* level, is eating a lot of apples a sin? How does one know, really, how many apples is *too many* apples? Whereas in Augustine (and the original Fall narrative) the law was external and conspicu-ous (a property line or dictum), in Baxter's version the transgression occurs *inside* the parameters of natural and legal behavior. This is consistent with the subcontractual character of the "law of grace," as well as with modern charges of Neonomianism aimed at Baxter; he imposed a new (*neo*) system of law (*nomos*) that entailed constant self-regulation and rehabilitation. It is in this discourse that Weber finds a tradition of capitalism-conducive self-discipline, but this soteriological reconfiguration illustrates more immediately why culp-ability remains so attached to illness and disability: With this reconfiguration, individuals are isolated from a form of disability that embeds them together in the human condition, but the connection between transgression and affliction (which makes each person "deserv[e]" their suffering) is retained at the individual level. In effect, Baxter imposed the rehabilitative possibilities of atonement on individuals themselves, calling them to find comfort in the capability they have been contractually granted by Christ. If fulfilling a lease is your forte, then this is undeniably a comforting reconfiguration. But we should remember that it was a redistribution of responsibility rather than an unqualified emancipation.

5 Diversity, Inclusion(ism), Discipline

While Baxter's attachment to a stabilizing ableism yielded a categorical aversion to disability, it did not require or entail an idealized model of the human body. On the contrary, his vision of the church celebrated physiological differences, and his ministry was built around differentiated instruction, aiming to suit support precisely to the needs of each individual. It is his 'inclusive' attitude, particularly as it coexisted tensely with the systemic ableism of his theology, that makes Baxter relevant to modern discussions about accommodation, access, and liberty. This is not as contradictory as it seems, either in relation to theory or to Baxter's own contexts. Theorists from Henri-Jacques Stiker to Jasbir Puar have demonstrated that policies of inclusion are driven by political and economic motives that are often masked, forgotten, or obscured.[189] Whether we look to the "handicapitalism"[190] articulated by Marta Russell or the "inclusionism" and "ablenationalism"[191] traced by Mitchell and Snyder, we can see how exalting certain tropes and forms of disability (often at the expense of others) can shore up geopolitical privilege, ideological legitimacy, and brand value.[192] Such tactics may seem too sophisticated for a seventeenth-century divine, but Baxter was intervening in debates of commensurable scale and complexity – about national identity, European power struggles, and political sovereignty. As I have argued elsewhere, the optics of disability inclusion figured significantly in religiopolitical debate, often as a means of marking the 'progress' of English Protestantism beyond Popish intolerance.[193] Baxter wrote more about inclusion and toleration than nearly any divine of his day, so it is worth examining how the motives and complications of his community-

---

[189] Stiker, *History*, 15–16; Puar, *Maim*.

[190] Russell, *Capitalism*, ch. 8; Dingo, "Mainstreaming."

[191] Mitchell and Snyder, *Biopolitics*, 4, 11–14.

[192] Albrecht, *Business*; Mallett and Runswick-Cole, "Commodifying"; Gill and Schlund-Vials (eds.), *Humanitarianism*.

[193] McKendry, "Blind," 62–64.

building procedures emerged in relation to disability. His inclusive policies were the correlative of his ableist soteriology, serving to formally bring the "New Covenant conditions" to "all the people of this Land," such that they would be capacitated for salvation.[194] In this sense, he embraced what Chris Mounsey calls the "Variability" of humankind; Baxter certainly cultivated the "patience to discover the peculiarities of each individual,"[195] even if the institutional ambitions of his project ultimately foreclosed such complexity. Since his account of humanity recognized diversity, his conspicuous circumvention of persons with intellectual disability is telling. Their marginalization confirms, as this section argues, that it was in the scalar gaps between ideal and implementation – when rhetoric became procedure – that the limitations of his theology became most visible.

Though Baxter's own experience made him especially aware of the intersections between ecclesiology and physiology, it was not unusual for seventeenth-century divines to consider the dynamics of ableism, albeit as they pertained to their own contentions over church practice. In divisive debates about sacraments and rituals, the normative assumptions about capability were often exposed and leveraged. The practice of kneeling at the sacrament, for instance, was sometimes impugned as incoherently exclusionary. Owen pointed out that "some Persons are lame, and cannot kneel," asking if a minister would really refuse them because of a "natural Infirmity."[196] The fact that Baxter made the same argument as his nemesis, claiming that mandatory kneeling unjustly excluded "a man for being Lame, or having the Gout in his knees,"[197] suggests the prevalence of this strategy, particularly since many church reforms involved prescribing bodily motions and rearranging church spaces. As Eiesland has shown, the inaccessibility of the communion table can exclude individuals with mobility impairments in ways that reflect a "disabling theology that functionally denies inclusion and justice for many of God's children."[198] In fact, the very barriers that Eiesland encountered in the twentieth century – railings before the communion table – were at the forefront of seventeenth-century debates; under the policies of Archbishop Laud, the communion table was relocated and barred from the communicants. Considering many biblical injunctions, such as Luke 14:13, enjoined churches to "call the poor, the maimed, the lame, the blind" to the feast, it is not surprising that contemporaries criticized Laudian policies on the grounds of accessibility. William Prynne complained, for instance, that "setting the Table at the East end of the Chauncell against the wall, and causinge the Communicants to come upp ... enforceth the people whoe are

---

[194] Baxter, *Aphorismes*, appx./107.   [195] Mounsey (ed.), *Idea*, 17.

[196] Owen, *Moderation*, 38.   [197] Baxter, *Reliquiae*, III.127.

[198] Eiesland, "Encountering," 584.

olde, blinde, lame, sicke, impotent to march upp to the Minister to receive, whoe shoulde rather come to them."[199]

Much of the incendiary debate over church practices concerned what was essential and what was indifferent (*adiaphora*), and Baxter himself frequently de-essentialized the policies of the Established Church on the grounds of accessibility. Against the universal attendance enforced by the Clarendon Code, Baxter repeatedly argued that attendance at parish church could not be considered "essential," either theologically or politically, since sickness and "lameness" prevented many from joining.[200] In a similar way, he brought various church practices into question by foregrounding the existence of disability. As for ordination by the laying on of hands, he invoked the case of a bishop who "was so lame of the Gout, that he could not move his Hands to ones Head, and though his Chaplain did his best to help him, yet I could not well tell whether I might call it Imposition of Hands when I saw it: Yet," he remarks, "I never heard any on that Ground, suspect a nullity in his Ordination."[201] Prescribing any practices without considering the variability of humankind, Baxter suggested, was not simply incoherent but potentially cruel. On many occasions he argued that enforcing attendance at Anglican communion (with fines and imprisonment) put those with mental "distempers" in a brutal bind: They would be driven to "distraction" (i.e. madness) by the strictures of self-examination. "Their dilemma is sad," he observed, "when they are either to go to *Bedlam*, or to the common Gaol."[202]

Seventeenth-century debates about religious uniformity, then, necessarily involved disagreements about the uniformity of humans themselves, and Baxter invoked the heterogeneity of humankind to impugn the monolithic paradigms and practices of the Established Church. As he saw it, "God hath not made our Judgments all of a complexion no more then our faces, nor our Knowledg all of a size, any more then our bodies."[203] "Among the millions of persons in the world," he gushed, there were no two exactly alike.[204] Based on this view of humanity, Baxter argued that it was "no more strange to have variety of intellectual Apprehensions in the same Kingdome and Church, than variety of temperatures and degrees of age and strength."[205] It is worth noting that tying the composition of the church so closely to physiology deviated from Calvinist theology, in which the church aimed for a more direct representation

---

[199] Prynne, *Quenche-Coal*, 29–30.
[200] Baxter, *Christian Directory*, 917; *Schism*, 18; *Church Concord*, 22.
[201] Baxter, *Reliquiae*, appx./35.
[202] Baxter, *Nonconformists Plea*, 184. Also, *Grand Debate*, 127–128; *English Nonconformity*, 148.
[203] Baxter, *Saints*, 526.   [204] Baxter, *Cure of Church-Divisions*, 348.
[205] Baxter, *Petition for Peace*, 10.

of the elect – a communion of the saints that need not so align with human physiognomy. From this perspective, we can see how the inclusive temper for which Baxter is often celebrated was based on a specific conception, application, and institutionalization of physiology. Though Baxter leveraged variability against Baptists and antinomians, most immediately this sensitivity served to impugn the paradigm of uniformity presumed by the Restoration Church. Precisely because humans were definitively diverse, possessing capacities as varied "as there is of persons in the world," outward "unity" (such as was purposed by the penal laws) was unworkable, whether assumptively in judgment or presumptively in practices. As Baxter put it in his officiously irenic *True and Only Way of Concord of all the Christian Churches*, one of his later attempts to redeem the failure of the Savoy Conference: "men are born of much *different Intellectual complexions*, and degrees of capacity: some are Ideots or natural fools; some are half such: some are very flegmatick and dull of wit, and must have long time and teaching to learn a little; and of memories as weak to retain what they learn: some have naturally strong wits, and as strong memories." In such a diverse world, no policy could produce perfect uniformity, whether by force or argument.[206]

Though such celebrations of diversity were often primarily strategic, this does not mean that they were insincere or inconsequential. Differing assumptions about capability necessarily figured in the far-reaching conflict over religious uniformity, and this dynamic emerged quite materially in disagreements over 'set forms': pre-written scripts for rituals and prayers (most notably the Book of Common Prayer).[207] Though the specific wording of such scripts was naturally a source of discord (one that sparked some of the fires of the Civil War), much of the debate turned on deeper disagreements about the nature and role of assistive technologies – about how much help an ordinary person should need. Set forms were often imagined as glasses and crutches, and as Mardy Philippian has argued, they probably made worship more accessible "for those individuals with limited, impaired, or simply atypical Theory of Mind, and for those with nonstandard language receptivity."[208] Human weakness was regularly invoked in such debates, but usually with a markedly dismissive or derogatory inflection; scripted forms were, many divines argued, "at best, to be used as Crutches to such as are lame."[209] But is using crutches a bad thing?

In keeping with his view of physiological difference, Baxter endorsed the use of set forms for characteristically conciliatory reasons, viewing them as a pragmatic device necessary for a universally capacitated church that would include diverse

---

[206] Baxter, *True and Only*, 81, 89–90.

[207] On the controversy over "forms": Maltby, *Prayer Book*; Targoff, *Common Prayer*; Como, *Radical Parliamentarians*, 384–408.

[208] Philippian, "Common Prayer," 153.

[209] *Sober and Serious*, 16. Also, Love, *Zealous*, II.54; Wilkins, *Discourse*, 19–20.

Christians.[210] The moral implications of such dependence hinged on how autonomy was understood, and in his definition of disability, as in his vision of medical care, Baxter asserted that dependence on "means" was entirely consistent with, and even essential to, capability. Not only did he argue that there was nothing essentially abnormal or shameful in their use, he also chastened those who dogmatically rejected such dependence; divines who "wickedly ... derided" people with "unready tongues" and "over-bashful dispositions" were ruining Christianity.[211] In defense of set forms, he often called readers to consider how incapacity was attendant on the vagaries of physiology and thus manifest among even the most mature and qualified divines. "Consider," he asks his readers,

> that there have been some very Learned able Divines (Doctors of Divinity) that by age, or other decay of Memory, or natural impediments disabling them from extemporate performances, cannot do any thing in the worship of God without the help of Notes or books; or at least without preparations for expressions; when yet upon preparation, and by convenient helps, they excell many extemporate men.[212]

When engaged with a practice that he prioritized, Baxter could evidently recognize not simply the variations of capability across time, but also the social character of disability; with appropriate devices, the apparently impaired minister outstrips the seemingly natural performer.

Yet, at the same time, we should not forget that normalizing such dependence arguably buttressed his paradigm of capability. As Sarah Jain suggests, generalizing the insufficiency of the body can ultimately obscure the inequities of technological dependence, naturalizing a "liberal premise of free choice" in ways that actually conceal disabled bodies.[213] This is partly why many are suspicious of the mantra 'we are all disabled'; while it is true that vulnerability and deficiency is universal and nearly inevitable, the needs and resources of individuals vary widely. Baxter arguably intended his figuration of set forms to mask such differences, especially as his "Levelling doctrine" challenged the paradigm of uniformity pursued by the Established Church;[214] he often invoked our common diversity to discredit alternative systems of support. Imposing the Book of Common Prayer universally, he argued, was like forcing everyone "to use Spectacles, or Crutches, because some are purblind or lame."[215] Such a policy, he contended, was at odds with the infinite variety of human capabilities, which necessitated a "special care and over-sight of each member of the

---

[210] Baxter, *Christian Directory*, 851–853.   [211] Baxter, *Right Method*, 447–449.
[212] Baxter, *Five Disputations*, 369–370.   [213] Jain, "Prosthetic," 39.   [214] L812.
[215] Baxter, *Grand Debate*, 74.

Flock." Where one individual might benefit from a scripted prayer "as a crutch to a Cripple," another might require a devotional treatise, and another might need public discipline.[216] A ham-handed national church policy premised on a presumption of physiological uniformity, Baxter contended, would be not only ineffective, but ultimately harmful.

But could a hyper-individualized policy demanded by such diversity be successfully implemented? After all, a system of highly differentiated support was only more effective and more just if the needs of individuals were actually met more consistently and fully than under blanket policies. In attempting to put his vision of boundless diversity into practice, Baxter encountered a dynamic that is increasingly apparent to researchers, policy-makers, and persons with disabilities: The injustice surrounding disability is rooted not simply in an ideology or environment, but in the disjunct between ideals of agency and systems of support, particularly medical and educational resources. His ministry was directly shaped by his optimistically ableist soteriology, which refused to "leave out any man" who desired salvation. Baxter therefore confronted the theological problem of disability in an urgently practical form: If "God would have all men to be saved" but expected them to do their part, how could the vast disparities of "natural faculties" be redressed – so that this promise was not specious or cruel?[217]

The pastoral initiatives Baxter developed offer an instructive attempt to address the interwoven administrative, pedagogical, and juridical issues attendant on disability. The ministry he developed in Kidderminster during the 1650s aimed to provide the kind of support that a deeply diverse species requires. Beyond his regular preaching on Thursdays and Sundays, Baxter spent Mondays and Tuesdays meeting with all members (often with his assistant Richard Sargeant), ensuring that each of roughly 800 families was tutored and every willing individual – from children to grandparents – catechized.[218] He reportedly spent an hour with each family, testing them and advising them on matters of belief and practice.[219] While catechizing was highly regarded in Reformed thought,[220] Baxter's system went far beyond established practices in persistence and penetration, such that it encountered disability far more intimately, especially as he combined his regular catechism program with house-to-house visits.[221] This was the least he could do; as he put it in his influential

---

[216] Baxter, *Gildas*, 85.   [217] Baxter, *Gildas*, 339.

[218] For summaries of his ministry: Black, "'Discipline,'" 658–673; Burton, *Hallowing*, 21–45; Keeble, "Ministry"; Lim, *Purity*, 23–52.

[219] Baxter, *Reliquiae*, I.83.

[220] On catechistical practices during the period: Green, *Catechizing*; McQuade, *Catechisms*.

[221] Though sometimes Baxter used this term as an allusion to Acts 20:20, in many cases he is describing a real practice (albeit one shouldered significantly by Richard Sergeant): see Baxter, *Gildas*, 420; L285, L768; *Reliquiae* I.88.

pastoral guides, the minister should know "every individual member" of the community because every person was unique. He should examine each individual in private (except women, to avoid scandal . . .), so that instruction could be finely suited to "their several Capacities." If they were "old people that are of weak memories," for instance, instruction was to focus on oral repetition.[222] Doctrines were to be ordered "in a suitableness to the main end, and yet so as might suit [the] dispositions and diseases" of different persons.[223] Baxter had an ambition to implement a version of this system nationally, which he pursued abortively in the Worcestershire Association he established. Involving five towns and more than forty teachers and ministers, this professional association sought to extend the disciplinary structure throughout the county with regular meetings, public lectures, ejection registers, grievance procedures, and best practices.[224]

Baxter glorified the "Government of the Body" and he often affirmed that a "fit body" was important, maybe even necessary, to serve God effectively.[225] So it makes sense that his system of discipline was intended to surveil and regulate not only the souls but also the bodies of the nation. The trope of the minister as physician was a commonplace of Christian thought, and Baxter regularly conceived of his own role in medical terms,[226] but the affinity with medical authority was more than tropological. Baxter served as the (amateur) physician of Kidderminster, his ministerial practice doubling as a system of "universal" home care – sometimes perhaps beneficial, sometimes perhaps intrusive, sometimes perhaps oppressive. Though he privileged willing and consensual conversion, he had no misgivings about the power dynamics that his position entailed, explaining that:

> God made use of my Practice of Physick among them, as a very great advantage to my Ministry; for they that cared not for their Souls did love their Lives, and care for their Bodies: And by this they were made almost as observant, as a Tenant is of his Landlord: Sometimes I could see before me in the Church a very considerable part of the Congregation, whose Lives God had made me a means to save, or to recover their health: and doing it for nothing so obliged them, that they would readily hear me.[227]

---

[222] Baxter, *Gildas*, 426, 422, 60–61, 433, 449.   [223] Baxter, *Reliquiae*, I.93.

[224] On the Worcestershire Association and catechizing: *Agreement of Divers Ministers*; Baxter, *Christian Concord*; Lim, *Purity*, 23–52.

[225] Baxter, *Christian Directory*, 447; *Right Method*, 365.

[226] Though he compared himself to both a teacher and a physician, he argued that the best "Simile" for the "Ministerial power and duty" was a "conjunct[ion]" of the two professions – physician/schoolmaster (*Gildas*, 326).

[227] Baxter, *Reliquiae*, I.89.

Baxter was a persuasive preacher and teacher, but he admits that his unusual success – and thus the promise of his practice as a model for nationalized parochial care – turned partly on merging education and medicine into a single disciplinary structure. The coercive features of this relationship did not compromise Baxter's austere conception of consent, but they do point to some institutional limitations.

Since it pursued a degree of inclusion and support comparable with modern liberal educational and medical programs, the sundry limitations – of resources, of scale, and of access – that Baxter's pastoral scheme encountered are illuminating. In his own parish, some residents reportedly complained that for this 'free' care Baxter's housekeeper took payment (in "Pigs & hens &c.") on the side,[228] and he eventually felt it safest to call in a professional physician. Baxter was exceptionally devoted and diligent, but he occasionally confesses that he could not keep up – that the "charge [was] quite too great" for him to manage.[229] While he initially took notice of every individual, ultimately he "could not afford time for such particular Observations of every one of them, lest I should omit some greater work, but was fain to leave that to their compassionate familiar Neighbours, and take notice myself of Families and considerable Numbers at once, that came in and grew up I scarce knew how."[230] If it had survived longer, the Worcestershire Association might have helped streamline some of this off-loading, and there were reports that Baxter's approach to parochial reformation had inspired other communities.[231] But the support that would be required to redress the "necessities" of every individual went admittedly far beyond yearly visits.[232] Even in providing the limited support they did, his industrious assistants were evidently overloaded, as they were expected to "teach personally, interlocutorily, & in smaller assemblyes," as well as to "visitt the sick, to admonish offendours, to comfort the feeble minded, baptize & break bread, & more publickly teach . . . " – and also to "deale with persons one by one in advise & personally instructinge the Ignorant ... [and] convinc[e] gainsayers."[233] Such commitment to the community was admirable but not scalable – not, as Baxter realized, without a sweeping transformation of financing, training practices, and pastoral administration.[234] In his criticism of the Restoration establishment (which put an end to his own pastoral experiments), Baxter highlights some of the challenges that attend his ecclesiology. Each personal conference was as demanding as a sermon in itself, and even five personal conferences per year would not be enough for most individuals. And there were many who were too "old and weak" to make the journey to the

---

[228] L1260.   [229] Baxter, *Five Disputations*, 317.   [230] Baxter, *Reliquiae*, I.21.
[231] Ibid., II.443–444; L285; L345; L768.   [232] Baxter, *Gildas*, 329.   [233] L333.
[234] Baxter, *Saints*, 541; *Humble Petition*.

ministers; they would have to be visited individually, else they would "lye and rot in their sins." "I have tried it," Baxter admits grimly.[235]

Pointing out such limitations – as we might similarly with systems like Medicaid or the National Health Service – is not meant to censure Baxter nor to naturalize inequities of care but to raise a critical question: In the face of such irreducible diversity, what kind of system would be necessary to legitimate a universal law premised on natural ability? The shortcomings of his ambitious approach suggest how disability can become a "problem" of justice at the scalar gaps between an ideology of ability, which imagines and treats the individual as morally autonomous, and the support provided in the face of variability, which regularly falls short. Baxter embedded his "ordinary" man in a "*World of means*"[236] that charged their power with terrible consequences, but providing the material support to legitimate such a system went perhaps beyond any human power.

The potential disconnect between discourse and implementation is especially apparent surrounding individuals with intellectual disabilities. As scholars like Simplican and Erevelles have argued, intellectual disabilities trouble paradigms of liberal education, partly because methods of measurement and evaluation are built around a limited (and historically contingent) conception of rationality.[237] Though seventeenth-century "idiocy" was not plainly commensurate with the modern concept of intellectual disability, the condition, when conceived as a radical lack of reason, presented analogous problems for Baxter.[238] He averred that salvation was available to "all men" and pursued this soteriology in his ministry, but his naturalization of rationalistic means effectively excluded those who outwardly lacked the faculty. Goodey thus suggests that Baxter finally cast "idiots" as "differen[t] in kind" – a separate "species."[239] Indeed, Baxter was in quite a bind, and dehumanizing "ideots" would have been the readiest solution. But his writing represents a more complex response, one more consistent with the liberal tradition to which he contributed. Though he often said that it is "our *Rational* faculty that proveth us men,"[240] he was not a straightforward "rationalist," as Sytsma has demonstrated.[241] From a modern standpoint, his conception and valuation of reason was comparatively limited, serving as a *means* to

---

[235] Baxter, *Reliquiae*, appx./100–102; *Answer*, 78.   [236] Baxter, *Gods Goodness*, 65.

[237] Simplican, *Capacity Contract*; Erevelles, "Signs."

[238] On the treatment of "idiocy" during the seventeenth century: Wright and Digby (eds.), *Idiocy*; Goodey, *Intelligence*; Hughes, *Invalidity*, 321–328; McDonagh, *Idiocy*, 79–151. Though "idiot" encompassed a wide range of capacities, Baxter regularly uses the term to describe a person "having not the use of reason from the birth" (*Christian's Infants*, 18).

[239] Goodey, *Intelligence*, 197.   [240] Baxter, *Treatise of Self-Denyall*, 280.

[241] Sytsma, *Mechanical Philosophers*, 71–104. On Baxter's conception of "reason": Burton, *Hallowing*, 72–79; Packer, *Redemption*, 103–152.

a disciplined community rather than its *end*. His attitude toward "idiocy" thus depended crucially on the context: He was motivated to set "idiocy" as an exclusionary boundary to defend practices like family worship or communion, but he was equally motivated to condone the baptism of "Ideots" to support his policies of baptizing infants, whom he considered to be "in the same case."[242] To emphasize the diversity of humankind, he regularly placed "ideots and natural fools" *within* the intelligence level of "men," situated among the "degrees of wit" that defined the human "species,"[243] and he implied that they had the same "humane nature" and souls as "ordinary" humans.[244] As such, even if they could not "actually believe" in the established sense, Baxter affirmed that "they may be saved by Christ" nonetheless.[245]

But how did this extraordinary process – occurring largely outside the programs Baxter so carefully implemented – actually work? Asking this question highlights how ableism can inhere at the *procedural* level even as it is repudiated discursively. Baxter did not exclude "ideots" from salvation in abstractly theological terms, but his semiotics of contracts and consent made them effectively invisible in the 'visible' church he implemented. As Baxter framed it, adult membership in the church (marked primarily through confirmation and communion) required a personal and public profession of faith.[246] In debating the complexities of infant baptism, he had developed a highly refined conception of how the "signification ... of consent" and comprehension worked.[247] The profession he expected was to be "credible," understanding, deliberate, voluntary, "seemingly serious," and consistent with behavior.[248] This sounds demanding, but Baxter was generally aiming to standardize and regulate rather than exclude; as he saw it, this approach would incorporate any who were willing and able, not just some contingent of the presumptively justified. Because these procedures were keyed to his normate, however, they demanded "a *Rational* creature"; a credible profession, he confirmed, could not be made by a "fool, or ideot, or mad man, or a child that hath not reason for such an act, no nor of a brainsick or melancholy person."[249] And he concluded quite clearly that "idiots" should not be admitted to communion.[250] Such exclusion was, as Baxter framed it, a consequence of semiotic limitations, rather than

---

242 Baxter, *Christian Directory*, 507; *Certain Disputations*, 9; *Christian's Infants*, 18. Also, *Certain Disputations*, 248.

243 Baxter, *Life of Faith*, 249; *More Reasons*, 129.

244 Baxter, *Directions for Weak*, 48. Also, Baxter, *Nature*, 10, 37–38; *Right Method*, 158.

245 Baxter, *End*, 215. Also, *Universal*, 455, 477.

246 Baxter, *Christian Concord*, B2ᵛ; *Confirmation*, 21–45; *Church Concord*, 14, 17–19; *Reliquiae*, I.114; L403.

247 Baxter, *Christian Concord*, B2ʳ.   248 Baxter, *Christian Directory*, 158.   249 Ibid., 694.

250 Ibid., 603.

evidence of damnation. But while this may have been a strictly procedural inequality, it nonetheless left "ideots" in a strangely liminal state, neither included by intelligible consent nor excluded by recognized refusal. The complexities and consequences of this position are evident in the way he compares "ideots" with parrots; they are incidentally (but not purposively) disqualified because their profession cannot aptly "signifie what is in the mind."[251]

In ways that recall the tactics of "deferral" and "postpon[ement]" ascribed to liberal educational and political systems,[252] the accommodations that Baxter developed helped legitimize the underlying semiotics of his procedures while putting off full inclusion for "ideots." Those with "backwardness or disability for public speech" (especially "some extraordinary natural Imperfection, and disability of utterance") were permitted to make their professions in private with the minister.[253] And he allowed written professions – sometimes perhaps even "broken words or signs" – to serve in the place of spoken, so that "dumb" congregants could be admitted.[254] Such cases, he aimed to show, would not compromise the instrumentality of his semiotics; he was committed to the "understanding" mind signified by profession, not the mere outward *"Matter* of the sign."[255] But those with "natural impossibilities of impotency," including "persons that prove Ideots, or [simultaneously] deafe and dumbe," represented an exception to the very word *"ordinarily."*[256] It is in the face of such extraordinary cases that his sensitivity to variability clashes with a commitment to standardizing procedures. His response to this embodied extraordinariness is not unlike that of Rawls, who acknowledges the problem of disability but "leave[s it] aside" for the sake of theoretical coherence;[257] Baxter surmises that *"Ideots* are in the same condition as Infant children," but he leniently "let[s] every one think as they see cause" on that issue.[258]

For a writer who systematized nearly everything, this is a remarkable concession, but it is consistent with the almost unthinking turn to capability that defines such moments. At the practical level, "ideots" necessarily exist in his practices, but they appear always in asides, parentheses, or undeveloped threads. Some of this procedural dynamic was baked into his foundational

---

[251] Baxter, *Certain Disputations*, 9, 4.

[252] Mitchell and Snyder, *Biopolitics*, 63–93; Nussbaum, *Frontiers*, 108–127. Also, Dolmage, *Ableism*; Price, *Mad*.

[253] Baxter, *Petition for Peace*, 67; Baxter, *Christian Concord*, B3^r.

[254] Baxter, *Certain Disputations*, 4; *Christian Directory*, 173.

[255] Baxter, *Certain Disputations*, 4.   [256] Baxter, *Confirmation*, Y2^v.

[257] Rawls, "Fairness," 234; *Political Liberalism*, 21.

[258] Baxter, *Certain Disputations*, 248. Baxter typically called for flexibility "on point[s] of mere ignorance," and he seemed willing to accept a "true [Yea] or [Nay]" to guiding questions about belief (*Certain Disputations*, 346, square brackets in original). So some persons with intellectual disabilities could perhaps have been quietly incorporated into his congregation (albeit not to confirmation or communion).

categories: His catechistical roll was based on a catalogue of "all the persons of understanding in the Parish," and he called for all children and servants "(that are capable)" to be educated.[259] In his formalized procedures, "ideots" and "natural fools" appear in the appendices, where their implications are foreclosed but their rights inarticulate. To the theologically troubling objection that "ignorance doth not wholly cut a man off from the Church," Baxter admits that "ignorance *qua talis materially*, is no sin (as in Ideots, Paralyticks, &c.) and therefore cuts not off," but reasserts that ignorance is definitively culpable in the capable.[260] But *what about* ignorance in "ideots"? How do they receive (or reject) the rights and responsibilities of the church? To say that such individuals could eventually be saved by extraordinary processes is to defer their salvation until heaven. Though they could theoretically be in the 'invisible church,' this was arguably cold comfort, not only because recognition within the parameters of the congregation was an important source of privileges and rights (and perhaps of educational and medical assistance), but also because Baxter contributed so significantly to the delegitimation of those very extralegal processes that this deferral requires. If Baxter yielded any territory to the alternative forms of expression and comprehension that "idiocy" can imply, it was only those hinterlands beyond the borders of his more humane order.

6 Melancholy, Means, Ends

If, as I have been arguing, Baxter's regulation of disability reveals some of the inherent tensions of liberal ableism at its foundational moment, then the fact that he is most conspicuously flummoxed by "melancholy" suggests that depression might represent its own limit case vis-à-vis the capability required by liberalism. Depression is currently among the leading causes of disability worldwide,[261] and its gradual destigmatization has revealed the inadequacy of existing health services and established conceptual frameworks. The intractability of depression would hardly have been a surprise to Baxter. Whereas the problems with strategically deferring the full inclusion of persons with intellectual disabilities may be apparent to us, melancholy was the condition that manifested most pointedly and irreducibly as a disability to Baxter himself. Not only did melancholy interfere with the will necessary to culpability, but its patent prevalence – the fact that it seemed so "ordinary" – challenged his presumption of a capable reader. His theology was geared for those "capable of knowing [their] own thoughts,"[262] but his experience often seemed to make

---

[259] Baxter, *Gildas*, a7ʳ; *Agreement of Divers Ministers*, 31.
[260] Baxter, *Confirmation*, Z2ᵛ–Z3ʳ.   [261] World Health Organization, "Depression."
[262] Baxter, *Certain Disputations*, 28.

the exception the rule, a disconnect that reflected back on his methods as much as on melancholics themselves.

The disruptive energies of melancholy emanated partly from its historical contexts, particularly in Calvinist theology, but the condition is also illuminated in complementary ways by transhistorical theory on melancholia and depression, which indicates why it might have troubled Baxter's early articulations of liberal personhood. Baxter was living amid, even at the center of, a national debate on melancholy, one that bears comparisons with our own.[263] As theorists from Michel Foucault to Elizabeth Donaldson have pointed out, mental illness unsettles liberal discourses "in which will and self are imagined as inviolable," as it represents, at least through secular medicine, a "symbolic failure of the self-determined individual."[264] Baxter, as we have seen, was glad to accommodate and adapt the parameters of capability so that they might include "every man." But melancholy, as Butler argues, "is the limit to the subject's sense of *pouvoir*, its sense of what it can accomplish and, in that sense, its power. Melancholia rifts the subject, marking a limit to what it can accommodate."[265] To be sure, melancholy and depression cannot be carelessly conflated, not least because the former was such a nebulous category even in the seventeenth century, when it was associated not just with "fear and sadness" but also with madness, psychosis, and gastrointestinal disorder.[266] But the complex filiations between seventeenth-century melancholy and modern depression are uniquely relevant in discussing Baxter, as his pathologization of the condition contributed to its secularization.[267] As Charles Taylor has argued, melancholy can be seen as an exemplary site of secularity, the "vulnerability" it once involved representing the "porousness" that secularization displaced. In cordoning off autonomy and articulating regimes of "counter-manipulation,"[268] Baxter contributed importantly to the "buffered" subject inherent to modern psychology. Moments of recognition and moments of failure in his therapy are thus telling. As indicated by the 2018 repackaging of his ever-current advice – *Depression, Anxiety, and the Christian Life: Practical Wisdom from Richard Baxter*[269] – what aligns Baxter with modern approaches to depression is the logic of therapy, which vigorously defends the self-determination essential to a legally autonomous subject. Examining Baxter's treatment of melancholy in relation to modern frameworks of depression thus reveals not that depression is a transhistorical or unmediated condition, but, quite conversely, that its

---

[263] Rose, *Psychiatric*; Solomon, *Demon*.

[264] Donaldson, "Madwoman," 107. Also, Failer, *Rights*, 29–55.   [265] Butler, *Psychic*, 23.

[266] Gowland, *Worlds*, 62. On the possibilities and problems of connecting "melancholy" and "depression": Radden (ed.), *Nature*; 3–54; Moody, 75–93; Schmidt, *Melancholy*, 8–17.

[267] On the 'medicalization' that reframed melancholy as a pathology: Gowland, "Burton's Anatomy"; Heyd, *Enthusiasm*, 44–71; Hunter, "Damnation"; Solomon, *Demon*, 306–317.

[268] Taylor, *Secular Age*, 37–38.   [269] Lundy and Packer (eds.).

sociopolitical construction is rooted in the reconfiguration of disability that Baxter helped propagate.

More pointedly and ineluctably than any of the impairments Baxter otherwise engaged, melancholy exposed the incidental injustices in both the logic and practices of his ableist soteriology. As the pronounced problem of melancholy was part of the broader tensions surrounding disability, it entailed similar exigencies, Baxter acknowledging the physiological reality of the impairment while prelimiting its broader juridical implications. The sociopolitical danger that melancholy represented, along with the normative assertion of rationality that might subdue it, is articulated in his "Directions How to Make Good Thoughts Effectual," where he concludes that

> diseased melancholy and crazed persons have almost no power over their *own Thoughts*: They cannot command them to what they would have them exercised about, nor call them off from any thing that they run out upon; but they are like an unruly horse, that hath a weak rider, or hath cast the rider; or like a masterless dog, that will not go or come at your command. Whereas our *Thoughts* should be at the *direction* of our *Reason*, and the command of the *will*, to go and come off as soon as they are bid. As you see a *student* can rule his *Thoughts* all day: he can appoint them what they shall meditate on and in what order, and how long: So can a Lawyer, a Physicion, and all sorts of men about the matters of their arts and callings. And so it should be with a Christian about the matters of his soul.[270]

The metaphors of unchained dogs and runaway horses were often used to explain the disorder of the Civil War, and their presence here evokes the natural hierarchy that melancholy threatens to overturn. As the professional figures (lawyer, physician, and student) indicate, what is at stake here is the order, health, and continuity of the social structure. Baxter invites us to observe the stabilizing effects of mental discipline at work.

But as it gathers energy, the passage opens up two different explanatory frameworks, a divergence that corresponds to recent critiques raised by modern Marxist and disability theorists. The "should" in the final sentence offers a pair of antithetical inflections: Though most immediately the word applies normatively to the Christian reader, who is enjoined to regulate their own mind for the sake of society, it takes on a more critical inflection as Baxter describes the condition. Here the gap between ideal and reality entails not so much an admonition of the reader as an interrogation of the world they inhabit:

> And so it should be with a Christian about the matters of his soul: All Rules of *Direction* are to little purpose, with them whose *Reason* hath lost its power, in governing their thoughts. If I tell a man that is deeply melancholy, *Thus and*

---

[270] Baxter, *Christian Directory*, 304.

thus you must order your thoughts! He will tell me that he *cannot:* His thoughts are not in his power. If you would give never so much he is not able, to forbear thinking of that which is his disturbance, nor to command his thoughts to that which you direct him, nor to *think* but as he doth, even as his disease and trouble moveth him. And what good will precepts do to such? Grace and doctrine and exhortation work by *Reason* and the *commanding will*. If a holy person could manage his practical heart-raising meditations, but as orderly, and constantly, and easily as a carnal covetous Preacher can manage his *thoughts* in studying the *same things*, for carnal ends (to make a gain of them or to win applause) how happily would our work go on? And is it not sad to think that carnal ends should do so much more than spiritual, about the same things?[271]

Whereas Baxter elsewhere hypothetically invokes disability to chasten his malingering readers, here this incidental denigration quickly becomes a frustrated critique of the very methods and techniques that he employed. The diagnostic focus, in other words, fails to remain fixed on the patient, and it is Baxter himself who appears troubled. Compared with a case history in which the epistemological mastery of the expert is maintained, this turn to exclamatory personal narrative seems to reflect what Ato Quayson describes as the scene of "aesthetic nervousness" associated with disability, "elicit[ing] language and narrativity even while resisting or frustrating complete comprehension and representation."[272] Indeed, the rhetorical questions that Baxter typically deployed to direct readers to their duty and to foreclose disability-oriented excuses now yield a Job-like aporia, which might be considered one of the "aporias of secularism":[273] a sudden yearning for a transcendental intervention that his own conditions of belief prevent him from endorsing. Melancholy evokes in Baxter a transgressive desire to break his own rules. The deficiency of his regular methods could be explained as a reflection on the general fallenness of the world – "the tragedy of all mankind"[274] – if it did not so self-consciously offer up his own locutions for scrutiny. From this disjuncture Baxter extrapolates a tragic vignette on which he invites the reader to reflect: While the hypocritical preacher exploits these mechanisms to great recognition and riches, the sincere Christian (the legitimately "holy person") falls chronically short, with the semiotics of holiness perversely exploited. As in the recent work of theorists like Ann Cvetkovich and Mikkel Krause Frantzen, the intractability and prevalence of melancholy suggests that it is not a mere "natural fact," but rather a manifestation of prevailing injustice.[275] This perspective generates an oblique critique of social inequality,

---

[271] Ibid., 304.   [272] Quayson, *Nervousness*, 22.   [273] Abeysekara, *Politics*, 34–83.
[274] Klibansky et al., *Saturn*, 80.
[275] Cvetkovich, *Depression*; Frantzen, *Nowhere*; Case and Deaton, *Despair*; Fisher, *Realism*; James, *Selfish*.

as the encounter with the melancholic reveals not a broken person but a broken system.

It would evidently have been most convenient to relegate melancholy to parentheses or appendices, but the condition forced itself into Baxter's life and writing in personally, theologically, and politically demanding ways. The cultural tradition on melancholy that Baxter inherited was "inchoate" and "heterogen[ous],"[276] and its threads – theological, moral, medical – were further tangled by his idiosyncratic position: an (amateur) physician, a (self-trained) theologian, and a (self-certified) counselor. Baxter was adept at weaving his own life narrative, but melancholy represented a knot that pulled together his physiology, his theology, and his politics. His account of his own illness, which was inseparable from his theology, was carefully developed in opposition to the condition. Baxter explained his "affliction" so as to rebuff the deeper vulnerability melancholy might represent. Though the "Common Talk" of London in 1674 ("especially the Women") was that Baxter was a "melancholy Humourist," he declares that "all [his] Life hath been extraordinary free" from melancholy.[277] Though physicians diagnosed him with "*Hypocondriack Melancholy*," he regularly asserted that he was "never overwhelm'd with real Melancholy."[278] His illness caused him pain, but he was at greater pains to prove that his will and self-determination were never meaningfully compromised.[279] We need not impugn his personal testimony to see that disavowing melancholy as part of his spiritual development, his authorial persona, and his political stance was an important attitude in his offensive against high Calvinism. Melancholy figured significantly in the battles over justification and ecclesiology that Baxter was fighting. In the schemas of gratuitous grace and unconditional atonement promoted by writers like Perkins and Owen, melancholy was an unproblematic or even auspicious condition, consistent with a proper and proportionate sense of divine justice.[280] As Schmidt points out, Calvinist theology figured despair as "a token of God's favor," such that believers were encouraged to cultivate and perform it.[281] From this perspective, melancholy might be a sign of election, the passivity it engendered functioning as humble attendance for grace.

For the theological, sociolegal, and even personal reasons we have already seen, Baxter forcefully repudiated this conception of melancholy. The more

---

[276] Gowland, "Burton's *Anatomy*," 229; Radden (ed.), *Nature*, 10. Also: Gowland, *Worlds*; "Medicine"; Klibansky et al., *Saturn*; Lund, *Melancholy*; MacDonald, *Bedlam*.
[277] Baxter, *Reliquiae*, III.173.   [278] Ibid., I.10.
[279] Baxter, *True Believers*, 59; *Reliquiae*, III.60, III.173.
[280] On the association between piety and melancholy: Gowland, *Worlds*, 159–161; Klibansky et al., *Saturn*, 75–81; MacDonald, "Psychological Healing," 103–104.
[281] Schmidt, *Melancholy*, 54–55.

ableist and laborious soteriology he propagated had no place for such debilitating sadness. "Spiritus Calvinianus est spiritus melancholicus": Baxter invoked the Catholic calumny to obliquely denigrate this feature of high Calvinist theology.[282] As historians have demonstrated, melancholy was pathologized partly by defining it as sadness "without cause."[283] Today, the phrase typically evokes an absence of social and environmental causes, such as grief, loss, or trauma. But Baxter illustrates a *theological* substructure of causation that had to be recomposed. For such sadness to be entirely "without cause," it cannot be seen as a phase in "ordinary" spiritual development; otherwise, chronically sad individuals might be merely righteous. To this end, Baxter systematically excised melancholy from nearly every aspect of religion – from the *ordo salutis*, from ecclesiological procedures, and even from theological inquiry. He considered melancholy individuals "unfit" for communion, since they could not confidently confirm their belief.[284] As for divine knowledge, he asserted that the "Melancholy Fancies" of "crackt-brained" enthusiasts were assuredly not caused by divine revelations. Perhaps most importantly, melancholy was *not* an appropriate response to divine law, for "it is a *cheerful sobriety* that God requireth."[285] The prioritization of self-regulation and capability are evident here; as Baxter saw it, sadness became "overmuch" when it affected "bodily Health," especially when it "disableth a man to govern his *Thoughts*."[286] Going far beyond physic and medicine, Baxter redefined melancholy, at the level of cosmological causation, as a pathological attachment to what should only be a limited and relatively short step in the ordinary and universal path to healthy faith.

   This invalidation of melancholy might have remained a merely theological preoccupation if Baxter had not been so implicated in the lives (and deaths) of melancholics. By his own account, he became (inadvertently) the leading therapist on melancholy during his day. He counseled innumerable "melancholy Persons," sometimes two or three a day, throughout his career, and he claimed that "few Men in *England* have had more advantage to know their Case."[287] As his correspondence confirms, he advised many melancholic individuals, such as Katherine Gell, for years at a time, providing spiritual guidance, reading recommendations, and even remedies.[288] Yet, the methods of such counseling were pulled between pastoral and polemical imperatives that were often discrepant. Since he could not allow melancholy to be legitimated as a soteriological step, he remained wedded to a rehabilitative approach that

---

[282] Baxter, *Two Disputations of Original Sin*, 10.   [283] Radden, *Moody*, 5.
[284] Baxter, *Grand Debate*, 127–128. Also, *English Nonconformity*, 148.
[285] Baxter, *Christian Directory*, 271.   [286] Baxter, "Cure of Melancholy," 266.
[287] Baxter, *Poor*, 16; *Certainty*, 171; *Reliquiae*, III.85.   [288] L534; L538; L990.

was often unseasonable, ineffective, or inadvertently cruel. This tension was especially visible because melancholics were among his friends, parishioners, and even family members. Baxter marks the opposing pull of these two imperatives in his "Directions to the Melancholy"; while he is motivated on the one hand by the "exceeding[ly] lamentable" case of melancholics, he is equally goaded on the other by the theological implications of melancholy – by those misleading divines who "exceedingly abuse the name of God" by ascribing theological import to "the affects and speeches of such Melancholy persons."[289] The former imperative called Baxter to acts of empathy and even recognition, but the latter required him to relegate melancholy to deviance and pathology.

Such multifarious proximity to melancholy troubled Baxter's ideology of ability, for it uncovered the persistence and prevalence of a category – disability – that he sought to unthink. Whereas his invocations of other impairments are regularly tempered by allegations of malingering and faking, Baxter considered melancholy as irrefragably "reall a bodily disease" as epilepsy or "palsie."[290] He acknowledged that melancholy interfered substantially with self-knowledge and "free agen[cy]," sometimes so profoundly that it maybe precluded self-determination. As he argued in "The Cure of Melancholy," the thoughts melancholics have "*they cannot choose but think*": "their thoughts, and troubles, and fears are gone out of their power, and the more, by how much the more, melancholly and crased they are."[291] For a system that hung culpability so fatefully on self-determination, this is a profound problem. As such, Baxter even came to consider the condition a category of limited moral exemption; since the culpability of personal sin was proportionate to one's autonomy, "the more it [melancholy] ariseth from such natural necessity, it is the less sinful, and less dangerous to the soul."[292] "Melancholy is a meer disease in the *spirits* and *imagination*," he explained, and "the *involuntary effects of sickness* are *no sin*."[293] Considering how carefully he elsewhere policed terms like "not able" and "cannot," it is evident here that melancholy challenged his most basic categories: Melancholics "*cannot* cast out their troublesome thoughts: They *cannot* turn away their minds: They cannot think of Love and mercy: They *can* think of nothing but what they *do* think of, no more than a man in the Tooth-ache can forbear to think of his pain . . . They usually grow hence to a disability to any private *prayer* or *meditation*."[294]

As for any theory of justice that is built around a presumptively able subject, the presence of such a substantial and profoundly "disabled" population

---

[289] Baxter, *Christian Directory*, 312. [290] Baxter, *Right Method*, 9.
[291] Baxter, "Cure of Melancholy," 270. [292] Ibid., 269.
[293] Baxter, *Christian Directory*, 318. Also, *Mischiefs*, 492; *Gods Goodness*, 46–47.
[294] Baxter, *Christian Directory*, 313.

discomfited Baxter's ableist soteriology. A vast contingent of mankind radically excluded from salvation by their unlucky physiology? That sounds a lot like predestined reprobation with an extra step. However, the broader juridical and theological ramifications of such a disability could be neutralized by scrupulously preserving the responsibility of the melancholic. "Responsibilizing" individuals for depression is an oft-critiqued outcropping of the medical model in its modern form, and Baxter demonstrates how this logic might be rooted in the proto-medical conditioning of salvation; to maintain the universal reach of capability, especially when individualized care falls short, any forces that complicate "natural ability" must be brought *within* the bounds of personal culpability. "It is you your selves that are the causes of this," Baxter argued in so many words.[295]

Blame can be apportioned in diagnosis and pathogenesis, as well as in relation to prognosis and treatment. Baxter typically located the agency necessary to maintain responsibility in the earliest stages, or the "beginnings or Approaches" of the disease.[296] Not only was melancholy often precipitated by some sinful excess, such as worldliness or idleness,[297] but the abiding possibility of self-reflexive self-care made each person responsible for their own prognosis. Even after melancholy had progressed, inviolable pockets of autonomy remained. Though terribly debilitating, the distemper, "like an inflamed eye, or a foot that is sprained or out of joynt," left many organs free for rehabilitative work.[298] To put it simply, "Melancholy disableth only in *part*, according to the measure of its prevalencie: and therefore leaveth some room for advice."[299] Partitioning ability into its own "room" helped Baxter to insulate it from all the complexities of agency and culpability that disability raises. His advice on the condition reflects this promise of self-partitioning. Baxter recommends that the invasive thoughts attendant on melancholic episodes should be steadfastly refused or ignored; shut the (metaphorical) door, splash some (literal) cold water on your face, and "*use that authority of Reason which is left you, to cast them and command them out.*"[300] As in his view of cosmological order, his procedural accommodations and adjustments reified an ideal body at the systemic rather than individual level. The "variety of means" God has provided, Baxter explains, is like the variety of the body itself, which has "two eyes, and two ears, and two nostrils, and two reins, and lungs, that when one is stopt or faulty, the other may supply its wants for a time."[301] The presence of such fit accommodations actually intensifies the responsibility of the melancholic, for they must precisely measure their activities to their fluctuating

---

[295] Ibid., 57.   [296] Baxter, *Reliquiae*, III.86.   [297] Baxter, *Right Method*, 14.
[298] Baxter, "Cure of Melancholy," 297.   [299] Baxter, *Christian Directory*, 304.
[300] Ibid., 304, 316.   [301] Ibid., 315.

capabilities. While "abateing piety in the main upon any pretence of curing melancholy" would be fatal, excessive exertion was equally dangerous: "marr not all by grasping at more than you are able to bear," Baxter warned, for "if a melancholly person crack his brain with immoderate, unseasonable endeavours, he will but disable himself for all."[302]

But how does the melancholic maintain the self-possession necessary to govern such precise self-regulation? It is at this moment that the developing moralistic tradition, which extends to modern counseling and self-help guides, must be obliquely underwritten by medical authority. Despite his doubts about doctors and his offhand admission that "physick doth seldom succeed" in serious cases, Baxter's first and "last advise" is "commit your self to the care of your Physician, and obey him."[303] These invocations serve to nullify the problematic imbrication of body and spirit, for the promise of medical treatment furnishes an inexhaustible reserve of unalloyed autonomy, and thus culpability. Since the resolution of this pharmaceutical promise is deferred indefinitely beyond the text, it is impossible to see how it could possibly fail. In effect, moral strictures make sense because the melancholic can always be capacitated by medicine – off stage, where the contingencies of care (access, cost, geography, etc.) are imperceptible. From Robert Burton to Thomas Willis, there were few writers who did not invoke medicine in their writing on melancholy, but in Baxter this serves a somewhat paradoxical role, formally conceding all efficacy to medicine while practically claiming all authority to moral counsel. By couching his directions within the bounds of medical intervention, Baxter preserves a moral responsibility that is indisputable because it is guaranteed by a medical promise that evades examination.

This imperative to responsibilize the seemingly "disabled" melancholic, whether in their shortcomings or treatment, visibly shapes Baxter's biographical account of his late wife Margaret, whose personal experience of melancholy demonstrates the promise of rehabilitation. Though it may seem uncharitable to suggest that Baxter uses the mournful *Breviate* to consolidate his normate, his account of Margaret consciously presents her as an exemplar to be imitated. Baxter may have been the first to associate melancholy with women and female weakness, as Schmidt suggests,[304] but it is Margaret's manly mastery of melancholy that Baxter focuses on, for this illustrates the universality of capability. As in his own disavowed brush with melancholy, a strategic readjustment of the diagnosis from the outset allows Baxter to fortify the remaining territory of self-determination. Though Margaret "called it melancholly ... it

---

[302] Ibid., 599, 153.   [303] Baxter, *Saints*, 414; *Christian Directory*, 319.
[304] Schmidt, *Melancholy*, 117.

rather seemed," he decides, "a partly natural, and partly an adventitious diseased fearfulness."[305] The "diseased *fearfulness*," however, involved the same mode of compulsion, Margaret having "little more free will or power, than a man in an Ague or Frost, against shaking cold."[306] There was no point in telling her to stop shaking; Baxter married her instead, and this union provided the foundation for a cure. "When we were married," he explains, "her sadness and melancholy," as he now calls it (at the moment of its disappearance), "vanished; counsel did something to it, and contentment something; and being taken up with our houshold affairs, did somewhat."[307] Considering the long-standing affinity between heteronormativity and able-bodiedness marked by scholars like Robert McRuer and Jason Farr,[308] the rehabilitative dynamic conceived here – melancholy cured by a good husband and proper housework – evidently taps into the naturalization of heteronormative desire. Indeed, it is this dynamic that has made the Baxter-Margaret relationship (even today) an exemplar of traditional Christian marriage. As one Victorian biographer put it, Margaret "gave her once giddy heart to the outcast invalid of forty-seven ... at first in a trembling diffidence, at length with an angelic courage."[309] Yet, Baxter did not exalt submission but rather self-mastery, or more precisely the self-mastery that comes by submitting to culturally authorized methods of treatment. The fact that Margaret "overcame" this affliction through customized counsel and doctrinally correct meditation demonstrates the durability of capability.[310] Though not all melancholic girls could marry Baxter, Margaret embodies the belief that even the most apparently incapacitating melancholy never fully disables.

Yet, even as Baxter showcased such 'success stories,' his writing on melancholy remains haunted by a sense that the condition adulterated capability in ways that compromised his normate. If, as Puar has recently argued, the "disaggregation of depressed subjects into various states, intensities, and tendencies" may force us to recognize the "limits of disability as a category,"[311] it is not surprising that in meeting melancholics so numerous and varied, Baxter's concept of disability crumbled. From the outset, his imputation of culpability was strained by the fact that melancholy seemed to effect the most righteous individuals equally or even disproportionately: "Pious and Credible" men like the minister James Nalton or Lord Chief Justice Richard Rainsford – "as Godly as any" that Baxter knew.[312] Though conscientious people could perhaps be prone to overexertion, like an over-sharpened knife or over-tightened lutestring, Baxter was often reluctant to reconstruct such blame, even if it was technically

---

[305] Baxter, *Breviate*, 44.   [306] Ibid., 76.   [307] Ibid., 47.
[308] McRuer, *Crip Theory*; Farr, "Queer-Crip Embodiment."   [309] Gordon, *Heads*, 58.
[310] Baxter, *Breviate*, 69.   [311] Puar, *Maim*, 25.
[312] Baxter, *Additional Notes*, A5^v; *Certainty*, 40; *Reliquiae*, I.431; *Certainty*, 172.

helpful to his ideology. Rather, his responses often obscure culpability, directing the reader toward corrective compassion: "these poor people," he remarks after anatomizing the condition, are "greatly to be pittyed . . . And let none despise such: for men of all sorts do fall into this misery: learned and unlearned, high and low, good and bad."[313]

His most intimate reflections on melancholy (which are, be warned, somewhat disturbing) mar his normate by breaking down the borders of the self that make "composedness" possible. "I know," he admits, "that the Disease it self is, to the Imagination, as disquieting as a Dislocation or Lameness is to a Joint: But," he remarks,

> there is some malignant Spirit that driveth it so importunately to Mischief. They are constantly tempted to self-tormenting Thoughts, to despair and cry, *Undone, undone*; and to think that the Day of Grace is past, and that they have committed the unpardonable Sin; and any thing that may keep their Minds on a tormenting Rack. And they are strongly at last tempted to destroy themselves: If they see a Knife, they feel as if one within them said, *Now cut thyself or stab thy self*: *Do it, do it*. If they go by a Water they feel as if one urged them presently to leap in. And often are they urged vehemently to hang themselves, or to cast themselves headlong from some high place. And, alas! many do it.[314]

Melancholy had long been known as the "devil's bath," the black bile providing a fit medium for Satan,[315] but Baxter attempted to strike a "middle way" that would preserve his agential subject from radical denaturalization. He averred that melancholy provided Satan an "advantage,"[316] but the fiend worked "perswasively" and deceptively, not by flat compulsion.[317] Satan could "do us no harm, nor make us sin, without our own consent or yielding," and he thus could not "force" anyone "to be bad."[318]

But the above description of melancholy goes well beyond "persuasion," so much so that the capability on which culpability hinges seems compromised. The discourse of "tempt[ation]" is intended to maintain this connection, but it is eclipsed by Baxter's dramatic reproduction of the overbearing suicidal ideation he apparently heard from his patients. The absence of any temporal or spatial alternative breaks down the perimeters of choice. There is nothing before or outside this phenomenon, for the impulsive voices follow the melancholic everywhere – kitchen and coastline, low and high, home and abroad. Baxter's

---

[313] Baxter, *Christian Directory*, 314.   [314] Baxter, *Certainty*, 171–172.
[315] On melancholy and demonology: Gowland, "Burton's *Anatomy*"; Schmidt, *Melancholy*, 64–77; Thomas, *Magic*.
[316] Baxter, *Reliquiae*, appx./61.   [317] Baxter, *Christian Directory*, 105.
[318] Ibid., 105. Also, *Directions and Perswasions*, 76.

advice, when discussing these same compulsions more than twenty years prior, attests to the baffling reach of the condition: Avoid being near knives, bodies of water, or "any instrument which the Devil would have them use in the execution" – in other words, virtually everything.[319] By 1691 (on the eve of his own death), his sense of such omnipresent compulsion had evidently expanded, for even sacred spaces are subverted, this domineering voice intruding "at Prayer, at Sermon, at Sacrament."[320] The agency necessary to sustain culpability inheres only implicitly in the continued survival of the melancholic, a circumstance that is constantly destabilized, not only in this passage but throughout Baxter's life.

Driven by forces that could not be assimilated to his ideology of ability, melancholy discovered the pretenses of his rehabilitative method and logic. This was a condition that talked back to his soteriological conditions, co-opting and distorting the techniques of self-regulation that he endorsed. Since melancholics represented a categorical disability, Baxter had a responsibility to "mak[e] them capable to receive plain truths," and his difficulty in doing so opened up a phenomenological gap between system and subject. "It will work," he realized, "not as it *is*, but as it is *received*."[321] Designed as they were for "ordinary" able-bodied Christians, established methods of reasoning, correction, and admonition were conspicuously inapt. "You can tell them *reason* against all" their melancholic fears, Baxter noted, "and so can I, and have done it as like as oft as most of your Curates: and yet they are Uncured."[322] What is so disorienting about such discursive failures, however, is that their phrasing frequently underscores our complicity with the incidental cruelty of ableist interpellation. It is we – maybe even "you" – who fail these melancholics. As he puts it in his *Saints Everlasting Rest*, "you may silence them, but you cannot comfort them: You may make them confess that they have some Grace, and yet cannot bring them to the comfortable Conclusions."[323]

Extracting specious confessions, upbraiding rustling leaves, admonishing a shivering man:[324] The roles Baxter has us adopt in encounters with melancholics are often most unflattering, since they expose how narrowly our modes of address are bound to an ideology of ability. Yet, these modes are the corollary of the ableist stance he characteristically invites his reader to occupy. This is the response to melancholy that is enjoined by a law that treats "every man" as inviolably capable. The dramatic failure of the means this law provides, such as meditation and self-punishment, makes visible their contingency, a dynamic noted by theorists from Freud to Butler: The performative self-reproach of melancholics exposes "the 'bans' of that society, its fundamental bonds and

---

[319] Baxter, *Christian Directory*, 54.   [320] Baxter, *Certainty*, 173.
[321] Baxter, *Gods Goodness*, 2 (itals. added).   [322] Baxter, *Reliquiae*, III.128.
[323] Baxter, *Saints*, 414.   [324] Baxter, "Cure of Melancholy," 266, 270.

demands."[325] Baxter was committed to the social and moral utility of such bans, but the metaphors that bubble up around melancholy seem to betray the ineradicable energy – dark, primordial, necrotic – that rationalizations and regulations masked. Like a carcass breeding vermin or a bloodless body with a "pulse and breath" of despair, melancholy expressed the corporeal monstrosity beyond the law.[326] Though disavowing disability required that the self be objectified so that one could study and treat oneself, melancholics so externalized themselves with such intensity that they broke down subject-object relations: By "look[ing] too long on the running of a stream" they made their "eyes misjudged of what [they] after look[ed] on, as if all things had the same kind of motion"; by "look[ing] too long on the turning of a wheele," they became "vertiginous, as if all turnd round."[327] But as materialists observe, everything *is* in motion, and the world *is* spinning. This is more than empty embellishment; Baxter acknowledged that melancholics saw something that was true but was simply too dangerous to know. They came to know "too much" about the terrible "deformity and danger" within themselves and beyond the laws and techniques that Baxter proffered.[328] In this sense, they saw the very instrumentality of these techniques, a knowledge that was not absolutely false but that had to be denied nonetheless – for the sake of self, society, and salvation.

7 Conclusion

What power or authority might bring these vertiginous souls back to themselves? When discipline, reason, even words failed, what force could unthink disability? Baxter began with words, his disavowal of disability imputing soteriological capability to "every man" and laying shared ground for modes of inclusionism that went as far as words could go. It was in the face of melancholy, a disability so ordinary as to be present in his own house, that the instruments of inclusion broke down – a failure that tells us as much about the normate of early liberalism as it does about the melancholics Baxter treated. When push came to shove, Baxter did not have a solution to the problem of disability so much as a solvent: an unequivocal appeal to the "absolute necessity" of personal righteousness. "Do not misunderstand me," he clarified when faced with such conundrums: "in cases of *absolute necessity*, I say again, you must strive to do it whatever come of it ... for it is that which *must* needs be done, or you are lost."[329] Exposing the unyielding divine violence typically mediated by the means and guidelines of the law, such cases authorized any and every degree of earthly violence – not toward each other but toward oneself.

---

[325] Clemens, *Psychoanalysis*, 90.   [326] Baxter, *Gods Goodness*, 2; "Cure of Melancholy," 267.
[327] Baxter, *Mischiefs*, 153.   [328] Ibid., 152–153.   [329] Baxter, *Christian Directory*, 315.

This is how Baxter foreclosed the most unanswerable implications of disability, sometimes even abandoning his otherwise careful considerations. "Though the Devil perswade you that it will make you melancholy or mad," he explained, personal faith was absolutely necessary, "for *without it*, you are far *worse* than mad."[330] If you would restrain and institutionalize your child or wife to protect them from harming themselves, why would you not use such force to preserve yourself?[331] When the discursive realm crumbled, as it did in the face of disability, it was such elemental violence that sustained the normate Baxter had constructed, cutting through every form of compulsion, from the political to the corporeal, with a Gordian blade. In this way, violence guaranteed human inviolability, safeguarding the tenet that one "cannot be *forced* by any one, or any means whatsoever." Even at the point of a sword or the barrel of a gun, one "may *choose* rather to *dye*."[332] But what if the enemy was oneself?

In 1687 Baxter received a letter germane to this question: Joseph Southmead, a struggling Exeter merchant, had killed himself, explicitly citing Baxter's *Saints Everlasting Rest* in his suicide note.[333] The news (along with a copy of the note, now lost) was communicated to Baxter by Thomas Morris, then Vicar of Harpford, who was astonished by how calculated and deliberate the act had been. After debating the morality of suicide with friends, settling his affairs with lawyers, and praying with his family, Southmead locked his chamber and shot himself in the heart with a pistol. Baxter had sometimes admitted that his admonitions could (and may) have injured melancholy persons,[334] and he recognized that some could be pushed to suicide by the same purgatives that humbled haughty backsliders. But the case of Southmead was the exact opposite: This was a man who had seemingly mastered melancholy and madness by destroying himself. "I think," Morris remarked, "it is the most deliberate selfe murther that I ever heard of, & it is the more to be taken Notice of, because what he writ, seems to have some shew of piety & religion in it." There was no way this could be melancholy or "distraction," Morris remarked.[335]

Was this the kind of inviolable self-determination that Baxter had called for? Morris sympathetically rehashed some of the arguments that Baxter had made against suicide, but the letter betrays the sense (expressed in the "ill reflections" of locals) that Baxter was somehow responsible. There were certainly moments when his calls for self-mastery overlapped almost perversely with endorsements

---

[330] Ibid., 311.   [331] Baxter, *Poor*, 14.
[332] Baxter, *Christian Directory*, 694. Here, as in many cases, the context for this stringent logic of consent is rooted in Baxter's experience of Nonconformity, which hardened his ableism by incentivizing him to exalt the inviolability of the will.
[333] Morris, *Morris to Baxter*.   [334] Baxter, *Duty*, 27; *Right Method*, 351.
[335] Morris, *Morris to Baxter*.

of suicide. In his *Treatise of Death*, he calls on readers to (figuratively?) "hearken to a temptation to self-murder" so that they can take the knife Satan offers and kill him with it. Such strategic self-violence might "kill your bodies, [but] it shall not be able to kill your souls," Baxter explained darkly.[336] In the passage Southmead had specifically cited, Baxter had indeed refused to condemn self-murderers, partly out of compassion for their loved ones. But there was also a theological imperative behind his outwardly enlightened response, one that prevented him from radically abjuring these "poor creatures." While a self-murderer indeed died with a heinous sin on their account, Baxter argued that their situation was not so different from that of every man; none of us were saints, and to require moral perfection at the moment of death would "exclude from salvation all men breathing."[337] To capacitate "all men breathing" Baxter thus had to yield capability even to those who stifled their own breath. Or to put it another way, to defend the universal ability to live imperfectly, Baxter had to concede the imperfect ability to live.

Baxter was reportedly haunted by many ghosts,[338] but few are harder to exorcise than Southmead. If Baxter did respond to this letter, the reply is no longer extant. And he did not, as Morris requested, "vindicate [him]self" with a corrective publication – a "little treatise … against self murder."[339] But if ghosts can speak through the living, it is fitting that the fatal passage from *Saints Everlasting Rest* was borne forward by that other advocate of "all men," Samuel Johnson. Nearly a century after Southmead had passed, Boswell vented a scruple that had been troubling him: If a man who had lived an upstanding life for seven years committed one transgression moments before his death, would he be saved? Johnson looked to Baxter, whose works he esteemed highly: "He will have the reward of his seven years' good life; God will not take a catch of him," he affirmed, and it is "upon this principle Richard Baxter believes that a Suicide may be saved." Boswell countered with Ecclesiastes 11:4 – "As the tree falls so it must lye" – but Johnson, after a moment of hesitation, explained that "*that* is meant as to the general state of the tree, not what is the effect of a sudden blast."[340] Johnson characteristically draws us out to the general condition of humankind, but we would do well to stop briefly in the aporia that struck him – to consider the unique position in which each tree has fallen. What acts of violence are necessary to maintain the ideology of ability that we have inherited? If, at its originary moment, the emancipation from disability required each person to become a "martyr in true Preparation and disposition,"[341] who is called to fall in the name of our faith in capability?

---

[336] Baxter, *Treatise of Death*, 69–70.   [337] Baxter, *Saints*, 97.   [338] *Life & Death*, 13.
[339] Morris, *Morris to Baxter*.   [340] Boswell, *Life*, II.457 (itals. added).   [341] Baxter, *Poor*, 31.

References

Primary Sources

Adams, T. *The Happines of the Church*, London, 1619.

The Agreement of Divers Ministers of Christ in the County of Worcester, London, 1656.

Barclay, R. *The Possibility and Necessity of the Inward Immediate Revelation of the Spirit of God*, London, 1686.

Bates, W. *Sermons Preach'd on Several Occasions*, London, 1693.

Baxter, R. *Additional Notes on the Life and Death of Sir Matthew Hale*, London, 1682.

Baxter, R. *An Answer to Mr. Dodwell and Dr. Sherlocke*, London, 1682.

Baxter, R. *Aphorismes of Justification*, London, 1649.

Baxter, R. *An Apology for the Nonconformists Ministry*, London, 1681.

Baxter, R. *A Breviate of the Life of Margaret*, London, 1681.

Baxter, R. *A Call to the Unconverted*, London, 1658.

Baxter, R. *Catholick Theologie*, London, 1675.

Baxter, R. *Certain Disputations of Right to Sacraments*, London, 1658.

Baxter, R. *The Certainty of the Worlds of Spirits*, London, 1691.

Baxter, R. *Christian Concord*, London, 1653.

Baxter, R. *A Christian Directory*, London, 1673.

Baxter, R. *Church Concord*, London, 1691.

Baxter, R. *Confirmation and Restauration*, London, 1658.

Baxter, R. *The Cure of Church-Divisions*, London, 1670.

Baxter, R. "The Cure of Melancholy and Overmuch-Sorrow by Faith and Physick." In S. Annesley (ed.), *A Continuation of Morning-Exercise Questions* (263–304). London, 1683.

Baxter, R. *Directions and Perswasions to a Sound Conversion*, London, 1658.

Baxter, R. *Directions for Weak Distempered Christians*, London, 1669.

Baxter, R. *The Duty of Heavenly Meditation*, London, 1671.

Baxter, R. *An End of Doctrinal Controversies*, London, 1691.

Baxter, R. *The English Nonconformity*, London, 1689.

Baxter, R. *Die ewige Ruhe der Heiligen*, Cassel, 1684.

Baxter, R. *Five Disputations of Church-Government and Worship*, London, 1659.

Baxter, R. *Gildas Salvianus*, London, 1656.

Baxter, R. *Gods Goodness Vindicated*, London, 1671.

Baxter, R. *The Grand Debate*, London, 1661.

Baxter, R. *The Humble Petition*, London, 1652.

Baxter, R. *The Life of Faith in Three Parts*, London, 1670.

Baxter, R. *The Mischiefs of Self-Ignorance*, London, 1662.

Baxter, R. *More Reasons for the Christian Religion*, London, 1672.

Baxter, R. *The Nature and Immortality of the Soul*, London, 1682.

Baxter, R. *The Nonconformists Plea for Peace*, London, 1679.

Baxter, R. *Obedient Patience*, London, 1683.

Baxter, R. *A Petition for Peace*, London, 1661.

Baxter, R. *The Poor Man's Family Book*, London, 1674.

Baxter, R. *Reliquiae Baxterianae*, London, 1696.

Baxter, R. *Richard Baxter's Dying Thoughts*, London, 1683.

Baxter, R. *Rich. Baxters Apology*, London, 1654.

Baxter, R. *Rich. Baxter's Review of the State of Christian's Infants*, London, 1676.

Baxter, R. *The Right Method for a Settled Peace of Conscience*, London, 1653.

Baxter, R. *The Saints Everlasting Rest*, London, 1650.

Baxter, R. *Schism Detected in Both Extreams*, London, 1684.

Baxter, R. *A Sermon of Judgement*, London, 1655.

Baxter, R. *Sermon sur l'Évangile de saint Matthieu*, Paris, 1664.

Baxter, R. *A Treatise of Death*, London, 1660.

Baxter, R. *A Treatise of Self-Denyall*, London, 1659.

Baxter, R. *The True and Only Way of Concord of all the Christian Churches*, London, 1680.

Baxter, R. *A True Believers Choice and Pleasure*, London, 1680.

Baxter, R. *True Christianity*, London, 1655.

Baxter, R. *Two Disputations of Original Sin*, London, 1675.

Baxter, R. *Two Treatises Tending to Awaken Secure Sinners*, London, 1696.

Baxter, R. *Universal Redemption*, London, 1694.

Baxter, R. *Wehkomaonganoo asquam Peantogig ... ussowesu Mr. Richard Baxter*, Cambridge, MA, 1664.

Boswell, J. *The Life of Samuel Johnson*, 2 vols., London, 1791.

Bunyan, J. *The Acceptable Sacrifice*, London, 1689.

Bunyan, J. *A Defence of the Doctrine of Justification*, London, 1672.

Bunyan, J. *The Pilgrim's Progress*, London, 1678.

Bunyan, J. *The Pilgrim's Progress ... The Second Part*, London, 1684.

Covell, W. *A Just and Temperate Defence*, London, 1603.

Downame, G. *The Covenant of Grace*, London, 1631.

Edwards, J. *The Plague of the Heart*, Cambridge, UK, 1665.

Eyre, W. *Vindiciae justificationis gratuitae*, London, 1654.

Ferguson, R. *A View of an Ecclesiastick in his Socks & Buskins*, London, 1698.

Fletcher, J. *The Historie of the Perfect-Cursed-Blessed Man*, London, 1628.

Fowler, E. *The Design of Christianity*, London, 1671.

Gataker, T. *The Joy of the Just*, London, 1623.

Hallywell, H. *The Sacred Method of Saving Humane Souls*, London, 1677.

Jerome, S. *The Haughty Heart Humbled*, London, 1628.

The Life & Death of That Pious, Reverend ... Mr. Richard Baxter, London, 1692.

Love, C. *The Zealous Christian*, London, 1653.

Milton, J. "Sonnet XVI." In J. Carey and A. Fowler (eds.), *The Poems of John Milton* (329–330). London: Longmans, 1968.

Morris, T. *Thomas Morris to Richard Baxter*, November 1, 1687, DWL/RB/2/5.140, Dr. Williams's Library, London.

Owen, J. *Moderation a Vertue*, London, 1683.

Owen, J. *The Principles of the Doctrine of Christ*, London, 1645.

Owen, J. *Salus Electorum, Sanguis Jesu*, London, 1648.

Prynne, W. *The Church of Englands Old Antithesis to New Arminianisme*, London, 1629.

Prynne, W. *A Quenche-Coale*, London, 1637.

Rutherford, S. *A Survey of the Spirituall Antichrist*, London, 1648.

Saltmarsh, J. *Reasons for Unitie, Peace, and Love*, London, 1646.

Savoy Meeting. *A Declaration of the Faith and Order Owned and Practiced in the Congregational Churches in England*, London, 1658.

Sober and Serious Considerations Occasioned by the Death of His Most Sacred Majesty, King Charles II, London: John Leake, 1685.

Taylor, J. *Deus Justificatus*, London, 1656.

Taylor, J. *Symbolon Theologikon*, London, 1674.

Tillotson, J. *Several Discourses of Repentance*, London, 1700.

Tillotson, J. *Several Discourses viz. Of the Great Duties of Natural Religion*, London, 1697.

Twain, M. "Advice to Youth." In C. Neider (ed.), *The Complete Essays of Mark Twain* (564–566). Garden City: Doubleday, 1963.

Ussher, J. *A Body of Divinitie*, London, 1645.

Wallis, J. *Truth Tried*, London, 1643.

Walwyn, W. *The Power of Love*, London, 1643.

Westminster Assembly. *The Humble Advice of the Assembly of Divines*, London, 1646.

Whichcote, B. *Select Sermons of Dr. Whichcot*, London, 1698.

Whitehead, G. *The Light and Life of Christ*, London, 1668.

Wilkins, J. *A Discourse Concerning the Gift of Prayer*, London, 1651.

Womock, L. *Arcana Dogmatum Anti-Remonstrantium*, London, 1659.

Yates, J. *Gods Arraignement of Hypocrites*, Cambridge, UK, 1615.

[Young, S.] *Vindiciæ Anti-Baxterianæ*, London, 1696.

Secondary Sources

Abeysekara, A. *The Politics of Postsecular Religion: Mourning Secular Futures*, New York: Columbia University Press, 2008. https://doi.org/10.7312/abey14290.

Adams, R., Reiss, B., and Serlin, D. (eds.). *Keywords for Disability Studies*, New York University Press, 2015.

Albrecht, G. L. *The Disability Business: Rehabilitation in America*, London: Sage, 1992.

Allison, C. F. *The Rise of Moralism*, New York: Seabury, 1966.

Apetrei, S. *Women, Feminism and Religion in Early Enlightenment England*, Cambridge University Press, 2010.

Arneil, B. "Disability, Self Image, and Modern Political Theory." *Political Theory*, 37.2 (2009), 218–242. https://doi.org/10.1177/0090591708329650.

Arneil, B. and Hirschmann, N. J. (eds.). *Disability and Political Theory*, Cambridge University Press, 2016. https://doi.org/10.1017/9781316694053.

Asad, T. *Formations of the Secular: Christianity, Islam, Modernity*, Stanford University Press, 2003. https://doi.org/10.1515/9780804783095.

Asad, T. "Thinking about the Secular Body, Pain, and Liberal Politics." *Cultural Anthropology*, 26.4 (2011), 657–675. https://doi.org/10.1111/j.1548-1360.2011.01118.x.

Balibar, É. *Secularism and Cosmopolitanism: Critical Hypotheses on Religion and Politics*, New York: Columbia University Press, 2018. https://doi.org/10.7312/bali16860.

Ball, C. A. "Autonomy, Justice, and Disability." *UCLA Law Review*, 47 (2000), 599–651.

Barclay, L. *Disability with Dignity: Justice, Human Rights and Equal Status*, Abingdon: Routledge, 2019. https://doi.org/10.4324/9781351017114.

Baynton, D. C. "Disability and the Justification of Inequality in American History." In Davis, L. (ed.), *The Disability Studies Reader* (17–34), 5th ed. Abingdon: Routledge, 2017.

Bearden, E. B. *Monstrous Kinds: Body, Space, and Narrative in Renaissance Representations of Disability*. Ann Arbor: University of Michigan Press, 2019. https://doi.org/10.3998/mpub.10014355.

Berger, P. L. (ed.). *The Desecularization of the World: Resurgent Religion and World Politics*, Grand Rapids, MI: Eerdmans, 1999.

Berlant, L. *Cruel Optimism*, Durham, NC: Duke University Press, 2011. https:// doi.org/10.1215/9780822394716-002.

Betenbaugh, H. R. "Disability: A Lived Theology." *Theology Today*, 57.2 (2000), 203–210. https://doi.org/10.1177/004057360005700205.

Bilgrami, A. *Secularism, Identity, and Enchantment*, Cambridge, MA: Harvard University Press, 2014. https://doi.org/10.4159/harvard.9780674419643.

Black, J. W. "From Martin Bucer to Richard Baxter: 'Discipline' and Reformation in Sixteenth- and Seventeenth-Century England." *Church History*, 70.4 (2001): 644–673. https://doi.org/10.2307/3654544.

Boersma, H. *A Hot Pepper Corn: Richard Baxter's Doctrine of Justification in Its Seventeenth-Century Context of Controversy*, Vancouver: Regent, 2004.

Breckenridge, C. A. and Vogler, C. "The Critical Limits of Embodiment: Disability's Criticism." *Public Culture*, 13.3 (2001), 349–357. https://doi .org/10.1215/08992363-13-3-349.

Bruce, S. "Differentiation." In M. Stausberg and S. Engler (eds.), *Oxford Handbook of the Study of Religion* (635–645). Oxford University Press, 2016. https://doi.org/10.1093/oxfordhb/9780198729570.013.45.

Burch, S. and Rembis, M. (eds.). *Disability Histories*, Urbana: University of Illinois Press, 2014.

Burch, S. and Sutherland, I. "Who's Not Yet Here? American Disability History." *Radical History Review*, 94 (2006), 127–147. https://doi.org/10 .1215/01636545-2006-94-127.

Burton, S. J. G. *The Hallowing of Logic: The Trinitarian Method of Richard Baxter's Methodus Theologiae*, Leiden: Brill, 2012. https://doi.org/10.1163 /9789004226418.

Butler, J. *The Psychic Life of Power: Theories in Subjection*, Stanford University Press, 1997.

Butler, J., Habermas, J., Taylor, C., and West, C. *The Power of Religion in the Public Sphere*, New York: Columbia University Press, 2011.

Calhoun, C., Juergensmeyer, M., and VanAntwerpen, J. (eds.). *Rethinking Secularism*, Oxford University Press, 2011.

Campbell, F. K. "Ability." In R. Adams, B. Reiss, and D. Serlin (eds.), *Keywords for Disability Studies* (12–14). New York University Press, 2015.

Campbell, F. K. *Contours of Ableism: The Production of Disability and Abledness*, Basingstoke: Palgrave Macmillan, 2009. https://doi.org/10.1057 /9780230245181.

Campbell, F. K. "Legislating Disability: Negative Ontologies and the Government of Legal Identities." In S. Tremain (ed.), *Foucault and the Government of Disability* (108–132). Ann Arbor: University of Michigan Press, 2005.

Carter, E. W. *Including People with Disabilities in Faith Communities*, Baltimore: Brookes, 2007.

Casanova, J. *Public Religions in the Modern World*, University of Chicago Press, 1994.

Case, A. and Deaton, A. *Deaths of Despair and the Future of Capitalism*, Princeton University Press, 2020. https://doi.org/10.2307/j.ctvpr7rb2.

Chen, M. Y. *Animacies: Biopolitics, Racial Mattering, and Queer Affect*, Durham, NC: Duke University Press, 2012. https://doi.org/10.1215/9780822395447.

Chouinard, V. "Making Space for Disabling Differences: Challenging Ableist Geographies." *Environment and Planning D*, 15.4 (1997), 379–387. https://doi.org/10.1068/d150379.

Classen, A. (ed.). *Old Age in the Middle Ages and the Renaissance*, Berlin: de Gruyter, 2007. https://doi.org/10.1515/9783110925999.

Clemens, J. *Psychoanalysis Is an Antiphilosophy*, Edinburgh University Press, 2013.

Collinson, P. *The Religion of Protestants: The Church in English Society, 1559–1625*, Oxford: Clarendon, 1982.

Como, D. R. *Blown by the Spirit: Puritanism and the Emergence of an Antinomian Underground in Pre–Civil-War England*, Stanford University Press, 2004.

Como, D. R. *Radical Parliamentarians and the English Civil War*, Oxford University Press, 2018. https://doi.org/10.1093/oso/9780199541911.001.0001.

Cooper, T. "Calvinism among Seventeenth-Century English Puritans." In B. Gordon and C. R. Trueman (eds.), *The Oxford Handbook of Calvin and Calvinism* (325–338). Oxford University Press, 2021.

Cooper, T. *Fear and Polemic in Seventeenth-Century England: Richard Baxter and Antinomianism*, Burlington, VT: Ashgate, 2001.

Cooper, T. *John Owen, Richard Baxter and the Formation of Nonconformity*, Farnham: Ashgate, 2011. https://doi.org/10.4324/9781315590622.

Cooper, T. "Richard Baxter and His Physicians." *Social History of Medicine*, 20.1 (2007), 1–19. https://doi.org/10.1093/shm/hkl081.

Coviello, P. and Hickman, J. "Introduction: After the Postsecular." *American Literature*, 86.4 (2014), 645–654. https://doi.org/10.1215/00029831-2811622.

Cragg, G. R. *From Puritanism to the Age of Reason*, Cambridge University Press, 1950.

Creamer, D. "Theological Accessibility: The Contribution of Disability." *Disability Studies Quarterly*, 26.4 (2006). https://dx.doi.org/10.18061/dsq.v26i4.812.

Cunningham, J. W. "'Justification by Faith': Richard Baxter's Influence upon John Wesley." *Asbury Journal*, 67.2 (2012), 8–19. https://doi.org/10.7252/Journal.01.2009S.04.

Cvetkovich, A. *Depression: A Public Feeling*, Durham, NC: Duke University Press, 2012.

Damrosch, L. *God's Plot and Man's Stories*, University of Chicago Press, 1985.

Davidson, M. *Concerto for the Left Hand: Disability and the Defamiliar Body*, Ann Arbor: University of Michigan Press, 2008. https://doi.org/10.3998/mpub.286540.

Davis, L. J. *Bending Over Backwards: Disability, Dismodernism, and Other Difficult Positions*, New York University Press, 2002.

Davis, L. J. *Enforcing Normalcy: Disability, Deafness, and the Body*, London: Verso, 1995.

Davis, L. J. (ed.). *The Disability Studies Reader*, 5th ed., Abingdon: Routledge, 2017. https://doi.org/10.4324/9781315680668.

Deutsch, H. and Nussbaum, F. (eds.). *Defects: Engendering the Modern Body*, Ann Arbor: University of Michigan Press, 2000. https://doi.org/10.3998/mpub.10866.

Dingo, R. "Making the 'Unfit, Fit': The Rhetoric of Mainstreaming in the World Bank's Commitment to Gender Equality and Disability Rights." *Wagadu*, 4 (2007), 93–107.

Dolmage, J. T. *Academic Ableism: Disability and Higher Education*, Ann Arbor: University of Michigan Press, 2017. https://doi.org/10.3998/mpub.9708722.

Donaldson, E. J. "Revisiting the Corpus of the Madwoman." In K. Q. Hall (ed.), *Feminist Disability Studies* (91–113). Bloomington: Indiana University Press, 2011.

Eiesland, N. L. *The Disabled God: Toward a Liberatory Theology of Disability*, Nashville, TN: Abingdon, 1994.

Eiesland, N. L. "Encountering the Disabled God." *PMLA*, 120.2 (2005), 584–586. https://doi.org/10.1632/S0030812900167938.

Erevelles, N. *Disability and Difference in Global Contexts: Enabling a Transformative Body Politic*, Basingstoke: Palgrave Macmillan, 2011. https://doi.org/10.1057/9781137001184.

Erevelles, N. "Signs of Reason: Rivière, Facilitated Communication, and the Crisis of the Subject." In S. Tremain (ed.), *Foucault and the Government of Disability* (45–64). Ann Arbor: University of Michigan Press, 2005.

Failer, J. L. *Who Qualifies for Rights?: Homelessness, Mental Illness, and Civil Commitment*, Ithaca, NY: Cornell University Press, 2002. https://doi.org/10.7591/9781501721434.

Farr, J. S. "Libertine Sexuality and Queer-Crip Embodiment in Eighteenth-Century Britain." *Journal for Early Modern Cultural Studies*, 16.4 (2016), 96–118. https://doi.org/10.1353/jem.2016.0033.

Fessenden, T. *Culture and Redemption: Religion, the Secular, and American Literature*, Princeton University Press, 2007. https://doi.org/10.1515/9781400837304.

Fisher, M. *Capitalist Realism: Is There No Alternative?* Winchester: Zero Books, 2009.

Frantzen, M. K. *Going Nowhere, Slow: The Aesthetics and Politics of Depression*, Winchester: Zero Books, 2019.

Fraser, N. "Rethinking the Public Sphere." *Social Text*, 25/26 (1990), 56–80. https://doi.org/10.2307/466240.

Garland, R. *The Eye of the Beholder: Deformity and Disability in the Graeco-Roman World*, London: Duckworth, 1995.

Garland-Thomson, R. *Extraordinary Bodies: Figuring Physical Disability in American Culture and Literature*, New York: Columbia University Press, 1997.

Garland-Thomson, R. (ed.). *Freakery: Cultural Spectacles of the Extraordinary Body*, New York University Press, 1996.

Ghosh, R. (ed.). *Making Sense of the Secular: Critical Perspectives from Europe to Asia*, Abingdon: Routledge, 2013. https://doi.org/10.4324/9780203111048.

Gill, M. and Schlund-Vials, C. J. (eds.). *Disability, Human Rights and the Limits of Humanitarianism*, Farnham: Ashgate, 2014. https://doi.org/10.4324/9781315577401.

Gilman, P. "Whatever the Sacrifice: Illness and Authority in the Baha'i Faith." In D. Schumm and M. Stoltzfus (eds.), *Disability and Religious Diversity* (19–46). Basingstoke: Palgrave Macmillan, 2011. https://doi.org/10.1057/9780230339484_2.

Glickman, G. "Protestantism, Colonization, and the New England Company in Restoration Politics." *Historical Journal*, 59.2 (2016), 365–391. https://doi.org/10.1017/S0018246X15000254.

Goodey, C. F. *A History of Intelligence and "Intellectual Disability": The Shaping of Psychology in Early Modern Europe*, Farnham: Ashgate, 2011. https://doi.org/10.4324/9781315564838.

Goodley, D. *Disability Studies: An Interdisciplinary Introduction*, London: Sage, 2011.

Goodley, D. *Dis/ability Studies: Theorizing Disablism and Ableism*, Abingdon: Routledge, 2014. https://doi.org/10.4324/9780203366974.

Goodley, D., Hughes, B., and Davis, L. (eds.). *Disability and Social Theory*, Basingstoke: Palgrave Macmillan, 2012. https://doi.org/10.1057/9781137023001.

Goodley, D. and Runswick-Cole, K. "The Body as Disability and Possibility: Theorizing the 'Leaking, Lacking and Excessive' Bodies of Disabled

Children." *Scandinavian Journal of Disability Research*, 15.1 (2013), 1–19. http://doi.org/10.1080/15017419.2011.640410.

Goodwin, G. J. "The Myth of 'Arminian-Calvinism' in Eighteenth-Century New England." *New England Quarterly*, 41.2 (1968), 213–237. https://doi .org/10.2307/363361.

Gordon, A. *Heads of English Unitarian History*, London: Philip Green, 1895.

Gowland, A. "Burton's *Anatomy* and the Intellectual Traditions of Melancholy." *Babel*, 25 (2012), 221–257. https://doi.org/10.4000/babel.2078.

Gowland, A. "Medicine, Psychology, and the Melancholic Subject in the Renaissance." In E. Carrera (ed.), *Emotions and Health, 1200–1700* (185–219). Leiden: Brill, 2013. https://doi.org/10.1163/9789004252936 _009.

Gowland, A. *The Worlds of Renaissance Melancholy*, Cambridge University Press, 2006. https://doi.org/10.1017/CBO9780511628252.

Grech, S. "Disability and the Majority World: A Neocolonial Approach." In D. Goodley, B. Hughes, and L. Davis (eds.), *Disability and Social Theory* (52–69). Basingstoke: Palgrave Macmillan, 2012. https://doi.org/10.1057 /9781137023001_4.

Green, I. *The Christian's ABC: Catechisms and Catechizing in England c. - 1530–1740*, Oxford: Clarendon, 1996. https://doi.org/10.1093/acprof:oso/ 9780198206170.001.0001.

Habermas, J. "Notes on Post-Secular Society." *New Perspectives Quarterly*, 25.4 (2008), 17–29. https://doi.org/10.1111/j.1540-5842.2008.01017.x.

Habermas, J. "Religion in the Public Sphere." *European Journal of Philosophy*, 14.1 (2006), 1–25. https://doi.org/10.1111/j.1468-0378.2006.00241.x.

Hall, A. *Literature and Disability*, Abingdon: Routledge, 2016. https://doi.org /10.4324/9781315726595.

Hall, D. D. *The Antinomian Controversy, 1636–1638*, 2nd ed., Durham, NC: Duke University Press, 1990. https://doi.org/10.1515/9780822398288.

Hampton, S. *Anti-Arminians: The Anglican Reformed Tradition from Charles II to George I*, Oxford University Press, 2008. https://doi.org/10.1093/acprof: oso/9780199533367.001.0001.

Harrison, P. *The Bible, Protestantism, and the Rise of Natural Science*, Cambridge University Press, 1998. https://doi.org/10.1017/CBO9780511585524.

Hessayon, A. and Finnegan, D. (eds.). *Varieties of Seventeenth- and Early Eighteenth-Century English Radicalism in Context*, Farnham: Ashgate, 2011. https://doi.org/10.4324/9781315548395.

Heyd, M. *"Be Sober and Reasonable": The Critique of Enthusiasm in the Seventeenth and Early Eighteenth Centuries*, Leiden: Brill, 1995. https://doi .org/10.1163/9789004247178.

Hill, C. *Milton and the English Revolution*, New York: Penguin, 1979.

Hill, C. *The World Turned Upside Down: Radical Ideas During the English Revolution*, London: Temple Smith, 1972.

Hirschkind, C. "Is There a Secular Body?" *Cultural Anthropology*, 26.4 (2011), 633–647. https://doi.org/10.1111/j.1548-1360.2011.01116.x.

Hirschmann, N. J. "Disability Rights, Social Rights, and Freedom." *Journal of International Political Theory*, 12.1 (2016), 42–57. https://doi.org/10.1177/1755088215613627.

Hirschmann, N. J. "Freedom and (Dis)Ability in Early Modern Political Thought." In A. P. Hobgood and D. H. Wood (eds.), *Recovering Disability in Early Modern England* (167–186). Columbus: Ohio State University Press, 2013. https://doi.org/10.2307/j.ctv17260bx.15.

Hobgood, A. P. and Wood, D. H. "Early Modern Literature and Disability Studies." In C. Barker and S. Murray (eds.), *The Cambridge Companion to Literature and Disability* (32–46). Cambridge University Press, 2018. https://doi.org/10.1017/9781316104316.004.

Hobgood, A. P. and Wood, D. H. (eds.). *Recovering Disability in Early Modern England*, Columbus: Ohio State University Press, 2013. https://doi.org/10.2307/j.ctv17260bx.

Holstun, J. *Ehud's Dagger: Class Struggle in the English Revolution*, London: Verso, 2002.

Howe, D. W. "The Decline of Calvinism: An Approach to Its Study." *Comparative Studies in Society and History*, 14.3 (1972), 306–327. https://doi.org/10.1017/S0010417500006708.

Hughes, B. *A Historical Sociology of Disability: Human Validity and Invalidity from Antiquity to Early Modernity*, Abingdon: Routledge, 2020. https://doi.org/10.4324/9780429056673.

Hunter, E. "The Black Lines of Damnation: Double Predestination and the Causes of Despair in Timothy Bright's *A Treatise of Melancholie*." *Études Épistémè* 28 (2015), 811. https://doi.org/10.4000/episteme.811.

Imhoff, S. "Why Disability Studies Needs to Take Religion Seriously." *Religions*, 8.9 (2017), 186. https://doi.org/10.3390/rel8090186.

Jain, S. S. "The Prosthetic Imagination: Enabling and Disabling the Prosthesis Trope." *Science, Technology, & Human Values*, 24.1 (1999), 31–54. https://doi.org/10.1177/016224399902400103.

James, O. *The Selfish Capitalist: Origins of Affluenza*, London: Vermilion, 2008.

Joshua, Essaka. *Physical Disability in British Romantic Literature*, Cambridge University Press, 2020. https://doi.org/10.1017/9781108872126.

Kafer, A. *Feminist, Queer, Crip*, Bloomington: Indiana University Press, 2013.

Keane, J. "Secularism?" *Political Quarterly*, 71.s1 (2000), 5–19. https://doi.org /10.1111/1467-923X.71.s1.3.

Keeble, N. H. "C. S. Lewis, Richard Baxter, and 'Mere Christianity.'" *Christianity and Literature*, 30.3 (1981), 27–44. https://doi.org/10.1177 /014833318103000306.

Keeble, N. H. "Introduction." In Keeble, N. H. (ed.), *The Autobiography of Richard Baxter* (xiii–xxx). London: Dent, 1974.

Keeble, N. H. *Richard Baxter: Puritan Man of Letters*, Oxford: Clarendon, 1982.

Keeble, N. H. "Richard Baxter's Preaching Ministry: Its History and Texts." *Journal of Ecclesiastical History*, 35.4 (1984), 539–559. https://doi.org/10 .1017/S0022046900043384.

Keeble, N. H. and Nuttall, G. F. *Calendar of the Correspondence of Richard Baxter*, 2 vols., Oxford: Clarendon, 1991. https://doi.org/10.1093/actrade/ 9780198185680.book.1, https://doi.org/10.1093/actrade/9780198185833 .book.1.

Keeble, N. H. and Whitehouse, T. "Rewriting the Public Narrative: The Publishing Career of Richard Baxter, 1662–96." In T. Whitehouse and N. H. Keeble (eds.), *Textual Transformations: Purposing and Repurposing Books from Richard Baxter to Samuel Taylor Coleridge* (97–113). Oxford University Press, 2019. https://doi.org/10.1093/oso/9780198808817 .003.0001.

Kendall, R. T. *Calvin and English Calvinism to 1649*, Oxford University Press, 1979.

Kittay, E. F. "The Ethics of Care, Dependence, and Disability." *Ratio Juris*, 24.1 (2011), 49–58. https://doi.org/10.1111/j.1467-9337.2010.00473.x.

Kittay, E. F. and Carlson, L. (eds.). *Cognitive Disability and Its Challenge to Moral Philosophy*, Malden, MA: Wiley-Blackwell, 2010. https://doi.org/10 .1002/9781444322781.

Klibansky, R., Panofsky, E., and Saxl, F. *Saturn and Melancholy: Studies in the History of Natural Philosophy, Religion, and Art*, London: Nelson, 1964.

Knoppers, L. L. and Landes, J. B. (eds.). *Monstrous Bodies/Political Monstrosities in Early Modern Europe*, Ithaca, NY: Cornell University Press, 2004.

Kroll, R., Ashcraft, R., and Zagorin, P. (eds.). *Philosophy, Science, and Religion in England 1640–1700*, Cambridge University Press, 1992. https://doi.org/10 .1017/CBO9780511896231.

Kudlick, C. J. "Disability History: Why We Need Another 'Other.'"*American Historical Review*, 108.3 (2003), 763–793. https://doi.org/10.1086/ahr/108 .3.763.

Kuppers, P. "Crip Time." *Tikkun*, 29.4 (2014), 29–31. https://doi.org/10.1215/08879982-2810062.

Kymlicka, W. *Multicultural Citizenship: A Liberal Theory of Minority Rights*, Oxford University Press, 1995. https://doi.org/10.1093/0198290918.001.0001.

Lamont, W. M. *Richard Baxter and the Millennium: Protestant Imperialism and the English Revolution*, London: Croom Helm, 1979.

Lim, P. C. H. *In Pursuit of Purity, Unity, and Liberty: Richard Baxter's Puritan Ecclesiology in Its Seventeenth-Century Context*, Leiden: Brill, 2004.

Linton, S. *Claiming Disability: Knowledge and Identity*, New York University Press, 1998.

Love, G. *Early Modern Theatre and the Figure of Disability*, London: Bloomsbury, 2018. http://doi.org/10.5040/9781350017238.

Luhmann, N. *The Differentiation of Society*, New York: Columbia University Press, 1982. https://doi.org/10.7312/luhm90862.

Lund, M. A. *Melancholy, Medicine and Religion in Early Modern England*, Cambridge University Press, 2010. https://doi.org/10.1017/CBO9780511674624.

Lundy, M. S. and Packer, J. I. (eds.). *Depression, Anxiety, and the Christian Life: Practical Wisdom from Richard Baxter*, Wheaton, IL: Crossway, 2018.

MacDonald, M. *Mystical Bedlam: Madness, Anxiety, and Healing in Seventeenth-Century England*, Cambridge University Press, 1981.

MacDonald, M. "Religion, Social Change, and Psychological Healing in England, 1600–1800." *Studies in Church History*, 19 (1982), 101–125. https://doi.org/10.1017/S0424208400009323.

MacKinnon, M. H. "Part I: Calvinism and the Infallible Assurance of Grace: The Weber Thesis Reconsidered." *British Journal of Sociology*, 39.2 (1988), 143–177. https://doi.org/10.2307/590779.

Maclure, J. and Taylor, C. *Secularism and Freedom of Conscience*, Cambridge, MA: Harvard University Press, 2011. https://doi.org/10.4159/harvard.9780674062955.

Mahmood, S. "Religious Reason and Secular Affect: An Incommensurable Divide?" *Critical Inquiry*, 35.4 (2009), 836–862. https://doi.org/10.1086/599592.

Mallett, R. and Runswick-Cole, K. "Commodifying Autism: The Cultural Contexts of 'Disability' in the Academy." In D. Goodley, B. Hughes, and L. Davis (eds.), *Disability and Social Theory* (33–51). Basingstoke: Palgrave MacMillan, 2012. https://doi.org/10.1057/9781137023001_3.

Maltby, J. *Prayer Book and People in Elizabethan and Early Stuart England*, Cambridge University Press, 1998.

McDonagh, P. *Idiocy: A Cultural History*, Liverpool University Press, 2008. https://doi.org/10.5949/UPO9781846315367.

McKendry, A. "Blind or Blindfolded? Disability, Religious Difference, and Milton's *Samson Agonistes*." In A. Conway and D. Alvarez (eds.), *Imagining Religious Toleration: A Literary History of an Idea, 1600–1830* (58–96). University of Toronto Press, 2019. https://doi.org/10.3138/9781487513962-005.

McQuade, P. *Catechisms and Women's Writing in Seventeenth-Century England*, Cambridge University Press, 2017. https://doi.org/10.1017/9781108182232.

McRuer, R. *Crip Theory: Cultural Signs of Queerness and Disability*, New York University Press, 2006.

Metzler, I. *A Social History of Disability in the Middle Ages: Cultural Considerations of Physical Impairment*, Abingdon: Routledge, 2013. https://doi.org/10.4324/9780203371169.

Mitchell, D. T. and Snyder, S. L. *The Biopolitics of Disability: Neoliberalism, Ablenationalism, and Peripheral Embodiment*, Ann Arbor: University of Michigan Press, 2015. https://doi.org/10.3998/mpub.7331366.

Mounsey, C. (ed.). *The Idea of Disability in the Eighteenth Century*, Lewisburg, PA: Bucknell University Press, 2014.

Muller, R. A. *Calvin and the Reformed Tradition: On the Work of Christ and the Order of Salvation*, Grand Rapids, MI: Baker, 2012.

Muller, R. A. *Post-Reformation Reformed Dogmatics*, 4 vols., Grand Rapids, MI: Baker, 1987–2003.

Nelson, H. F. and Alker, S. "'Perfect According to Their Kind': Deformity, Defect, and Disease in the Natural Philosophy of Margaret Cavendish." In C. Mounsey (ed.), *The Idea of Disability in the Eighteenth Century* (31–47). Lewisburg, PA: Bucknell University Press, 2014.

Nielsen, K. E. *A Disability History of the United States*, Boston: Beacon, 2012.

Nussbaum, M. C. *Frontiers of Justice: Disability, Nationality, Species Membership*, Cambridge, MA: Harvard University Press, 2006. https://doi.org/10.2307/j.ctv1c7zftw.

Nuttall, G. F. *Richard Baxter and Philip Doddridge: A Study in a Tradition*, Oxford University Press, 1951.

Nuttall, G. F., Thomas, R., Whitehorn, R. D., and Lismer Short, H. *The Beginnings of Nonconformity*, London: James Clarke, 1964.

Olyan, S. M. *Disability in the Hebrew Bible: Interpreting Mental and Physical Differences*, Cambridge University Press, 2008. https://doi.org/10.1017/CBO9780511499036.

Packer, J. I. *A Quest for Godliness: The Puritan Vision of the Christian Life*, Wheaton, IL: Crossway, 1990.

Packer, J. I. *The Redemption & Restoration of Man in the Thought of Richard Baxter*, Vancouver: Regent, 2003.

Parsons, T. *Societies: Evolutionary and Comparative Perspectives*, Englewood Cliffs, NJ: Prentice-Hall, 1966.

Pearson, J. "Disabled Rites? Ritual and Disability in Wicca." In D. Schumm and M. Stoltzfus (eds.), *Disability and Religious Diversity* (75–90). Basingstoke: Palgrave Macmillan, 2011. https://doi.org/10.1057/9780230339484_4.

Philippian, M. "The Book of Common Prayer, Theory of Mind, and Autism in Early Modern England." In A. P. Hobgood and D. H. Wood (eds.), *Recovering Disability in Early Modern England* (150–166). Columbus: Ohio State University Press, 2013. https://doi.org/10.2307/j.ctv17260bx.14.

Pinheiro, L. G. "The Ableist Contract: Intellectual Disability and the Limits of Justice in Kant's Political Thought." In B. Arneil and N. J. Hirschmann (eds.), *Disability and Political Theory* (43–78). Cambridge University Press, 2016. https://doi.org/10.1017/9781316694053.004.

Placher, W. C. *The Domestication of Transcendence*, Louisville, KT: Westminster John Knox, 1996.

Price, M. *Mad at School: Rhetorics of Mental Disability and Academic Life*, Ann Arbor: University of Michigan Press, 2011. https://doi.org/10.3998/mpub.1612837.

Puar, J. K. *The Right to Maim: Debility, Capacity, Disability*, Durham, NC: Duke University Press, 2017. https://doi.org/10.1515/9780822372530.

Quayson, A. *Aesthetic Nervousness: Disability and the Crisis of Representation*, New York: Columbia University Press, 2007.

Radden, J. *Moody Minds Distempered: Essays on Melancholy and Depression*, Oxford University Press, 2009. https://doi.org/10.1093/acprof:oso/9780195151657.001.0001.

Radden, J. (ed.). *The Nature of Melancholy: From Aristotle to Kristeva*, Oxford University Press, 2000.

Rawls, J. "Justice as Fairness: Political not Metaphysical." *Philosophy & Public Affairs*, 14.3 (1985), 233–251.

Rawls, J. *Political Liberalism*, New York: Columbia University Press, 1996.

Rembis, M., Kudlick, C., and Nielsen, K. (eds.). *The Oxford Handbook of Disability History*, Oxford University Press, 2018. https://doi.org/10.1093/oxfordhb/9780190234959.001.0001.

Reynolds, T. E. *Vulnerable Communion: A Theology of Disability and Hospitality*, Grand Rapids, MI: Brazos Press, 2008.

Riddle, C. A. (ed.). *From Disability Theory to Practice*, Lanham, MA: Lexington, 2018.

Rivers, I. *Reason, Grace, and Sentiment: A Study of the Language of Religion and Ethics in England, 1660–1780*, vol. 1, Cambridge University Press, 1991.

Rose, N. *Our Psychiatric Future: The Politics of Mental Health*, Cambridge: Polity, 2019.

Round, P. H. *Removable Type: Histories of the Book in Indian Country, 1663–1880*, Chapel Hill: University of North Carolina Press, 2010. https://doi.org/10.5149/9780807899472_round.

Rubin, J. H. *Religious Melancholy and Protestant Experience in America*, Oxford University Press, 1994.

Russell, M. *Capitalism & Disability*, K. Rosenthal (ed.), Chicago: Haymarket, 2019.

Sandel, M. J. "The Procedural Republic and the Unencumbered Self." *Political Theory*, 12.1 (1984), 81–96. https://doi.org/10.1177/0090591784012001005.

Scheer, M., Fadil, N., and Johnson, B. S. (eds.). *Secular Bodies, Affects and Emotions*, London: Bloomsbury, 2019. http://doi.org/10.5040/9781350065253.

Schipper, J. *Disability Studies and the Hebrew Bible*, London: T&T Clark, 2006.

Schmidt, J. *Melancholy and the Care of the Soul: Religion, Moral Philosophy and Madness in Early Modern England*, Aldershot: Ashgate, 2007. https://doi.org/10.4324/9781315249209.

Schumm, D. and Stoltzfus, M. (eds.). *Disability and Religious Diversity*, Basingstoke: Palgrave Macmillan, 2011. https://doi.org/10.1057/9780230339484.

Schumm, D. and Stoltzfus, M. (eds.). *Disability in Judaism, Christianity, and Islam: Sacred Texts, Historical Traditions, and Social Analysis*, Basingstoke: Palgrave Macmillan, 2011. https://doi.org/10.1057/9780230339491.

Shildrick, M. *Leaky Bodies and Boundaries: Feminism, Postmodernism and (Bio)ethics*, Abingdon: Routledge, 1997. https://doi.org/10.4324/9781315004952.

Siebers, T. *Disability Theory*, Ann Arbor: University of Michigan Press, 2008. https://doi.org/10.3998/mpub.309723.

Silvers, A. and Francis, L. P. "Justice through Trust: Disability and the 'Outlier Problem' in Social Contract Theory." *Ethics*, 116.1 (2005), 40–76. https://doi.org/10.1086/454368.

Simplican, S. C. *The Capacity Contract: Intellectual Disability and the Question of Citizenship*, Minneapolis: University of Minnesota Press, 2015. https://doi.org/10.5749/minnesota/9780816693979.001.0001.

Singer, J. "Disability and the Social Body." *postmedieval*, 3.2 (2012), 135–141. https://doi.org/10.1057/pmed.2012.15.

Solomon, A. *The Noonday Demon: An Atlas of Depression*, New York: Scribner, 2001.

Spurr, J. *Restoration Church of England, 1646–1689*, New Haven, CT: Yale University Press, 1991. https://doi.org/10.2307/j.ctt211qx3d.

Stark, R. "Secularization, RIP." *Sociology of Religion*, 60.3 (1999), 249–273. https://doi.org/10.2307/3711936.

Steele, L. and Thomas, S. (eds.). "Disability at the Peripheries." Special issue, *Griffith Law Review*, 23.3 (2014).

Stiker, H.-J. *A History of Disability*, Ann Arbor: University of Michigan Press, 1999. https://doi.org/10.3998/mpub.11575987.

Stout, J. *Democracy and Tradition*, Princeton University Press, 2004.

Sytsma, D. S. *Richard Baxter and the Mechanical Philosophers*, Oxford University Press, 2017. https://doi.org/10.1093/acprof:oso/9780190274870.001.0001.

Targoff, R. *Common Prayer: The Language of Public Devotion in Early Modern England*, University of Chicago Press, 2001.

Taylor, C. *A Secular Age*, Cambridge, MA: Harvard University Press, 2007.

Thomas, K. *Religion and the Decline of Magic*, New York: Scribner, 1971.

Tomalin, E. "Religion and a Rights-Based Approach to Development." *Progress in Development Studies*, 6.2 (2006), 93–108. https://doi.org/10.1191/1464993406ps130oa.

Trueman, C. R. "Reformed Orthodoxy in Britain." *Southern Baptist Journal of Theology*, 14.4 (2010), 4–18.

Trueman, C. R. "Richard Baxter on Christian Unity," *Westminster Theological Journal*, 61 (1999), 53–71.

Turner, D. M. *Disability in Eighteenth-Century England: Imagining Physical Impairment*, Abingdon: Routledge, 2012. https://doi.org/10.4324/9780203117545.

Turner, D. M. and Stagg, K. (eds.). *Social Histories of Disability and Deformity*, Abingdon: Routledge, 2006. https://doi.org/10.4324/9780203008522.

Tyacke, N. *Anti-Calvinists: The Rise of English Arminianism, c. 1590–1640*, Oxford: Clarendon, 1987. https://doi.org/10.1093/acprof:oso/9780198201847.001.0001.

Tyacke, N. "Puritanism, Arminianism and Counter-Revolution." In C. Russell (ed.), *The Origins of the English Civil War* (119–143). Basingstoke: Macmillan, 1973. https://doi.org/10.1007/978-1-349-15496-8_5.

Wallace, D. D. *Puritans and Predestination: Grace in English Protestant Theology, 1525–1695*, Chapel Hill: University of North Carolina Press, 1982.

Wallace, D. D. *Shapers of English Calvinism, 1660–1714*, Oxford University Press, 2011. https://doi.org/10.1093/acprof:oso/9780199744831.001.0001.

Warner, M., VanAntwerpen, J., and Calhoun, C. (eds.). *Varieties of Secularism in a Secular Age*, Cambridge, MA: Harvard University Press, 2010.

Warner, R. *Secularization and Its Discontents*, London: Continuum, 2010. https://doi.org/10.5040/9781472549341.

Weber, M. *The Protestant Ethic and the Spirit of Capitalism*, T. Parsons, trans., London: Allen & Unwin, 1930.

Webster, T. *Godly Clergy in Early Stuart England: The Caroline Puritan Movement, c. 1620–1643*, Cambridge University Press, 1997. https://doi.org/10.1017/CBO9780511583186.

Wendell, S. "Unhealthy Disabled: Treating Chronic Illnesses as Disabilities." *Hypatia*, 16.4 (2001), 17–33. https://doi.org/10.1111/j.1527-2001.2001.tb00751.x.

Wheatley, E. *Stumbling Blocks before the Blind: Medieval Constructions of a Disability*, Ann Arbor: University of Michigan Press, 2010. https://doi.org/10.3998/mpub.915892.

World Health Organization. "Depression." 2020. www.who.int/news-room/fact-sheets/detail/depression.

Williams, K. S. "Enabling Richard: The Rhetoric of Disability in *Richard III*." *Disability Studies Quarterly*, 29.4 (2009).

Wilson, J. R. "The Trouble with Disability in Shakespeare Studies." *Disability Studies Quarterly*, 37.2 (2017).

Wolbring, G. "The Politics of Ableism." *Development*, 51.2 (2008), 252–258. https://doi.org/10.1057/dev.2008.17.

Wong, S. I. "Duties of Justice to Citizens with Cognitive Disabilities." *Metaphilosophy*, 40.3/4 (2009), 382–401. https://doi.org/10.1111/j.1467-9973.2009.01604.x.

Wood, D. H. "Staging Disability in Renaissance Drama." In A. F. Kinney and T. W. Hopper (eds.), *A New Companion to Renaissance Drama* (487–500). Hoboken: Wiley-Blackwell, 2017. https://doi.org/10.1002/9781118824016.ch34.

Wright, D. and Digby, A. (eds.). *From Idiocy to Mental Deficiency: Historical Perspectives on People with Learning Disabilities*, Abingdon: Routledge, 1996. https://doi.org/10.4324/9780203162248.

Yong, A. *Theology and Down Syndrome: Reimagining Disability in Late Modernity*, Waco, TX: Baylor University Press, 2007.

Zuckerman, P. and Shook, J. R. (eds.). *The Oxford Handbook of Secularism*, Oxford University Press, 2017. https://doi.org/10.1093/oxfordhb/9780199988457.001.0001.

Acknowledgements

I am grateful for the assistance and resources of various libraries, including Nord University, Yale University, and McMaster University, as well as Dr. Williams' Library and the Thomas Fisher Rare Book Library. Parts of this project have been funded by the Social Sciences and Humanities Research Council of Canada, the Nord Open Access Fund, and the Faculty of Education and Arts at Nord University. Several generous colleagues and friends have provided valuable advice and support throughout the development of this project, in particular Stephen Ahern, Jamie Callison, Alison Conway, Tim Cooper, Meghan Freeman, Thomas Keymer, Timothy Kreiner, Katja Lindskog, Joseph North, and Peter Walmsley. This Element would have been far less lucid and accessible without the critical commentary of the series editors, Rebecca Bullard and Eve Bannet, the precision of the production team at Cambridge University Press, and the insight of the thoughtful readers. Without the patience and perspective of my brilliant wife Heather, who has come (unwillingly) to know Baxter so well, this project would have been little more than some haphazard reflections. And thanks especially to Bjørn.

About the Author

Andrew McKendry is Associate Professor of English Literature at Nord University. His work focuses on Protestant Dissent, religious difference, and disability in seventeenth- and eighteenth-century England. He has published on John Milton, Daniel Defoe, and Mary Wollstonecraft, and his work has appeared in journals such as *Eighteenth-Century Studies* and *Studies in Romanticism*. He leads the Humanities, Education and Culture Research Group at Nord, where he also teaches classes on literary theory, pedagogy, environmental humanities, and the cultural history of the Long Eighteenth Century.

Cambridge Elements ≡

Eighteenth-Century Connections

Series Editors

Eve Tavor Bannet
University of Oklahoma

Eve Tavor Bannet is George Lynn Cross Professor Emeritus, University of Oklahoma and editor of *Studies in Eighteenth-Century Culture*. Her monographs include *Empire of Letters: Letter Manuals and Transatlantic Correspondence 1688–1820* (Cambridge, 2005), *Transatlantic Stories and the History of Reading, 1720–1820* (Cambridge, 2011), and *Eighteenth-Century Manners of Reading: Print Culture and Popular Instruction in the Anglophone Atlantic World* (Cambridge, 2017). She is editor of *British and American Letter Manuals 1680–1810* (Pickering & Chatto, 2008), *Emma Corbett* (Broadview, 2011) and, with Susan Manning, *Transatlantic Literary Studies* (Cambridge, 2012).

Rebecca Bullard
University of Reading

Rebecca Bullard is Associate Professor of English Literature at the University of Reading. She is the author of *The Politics of Disclosure: Secret History Narratives, 1674–1725* (Pickering & Chatto, 2009), co-editor of *The Plays and Poems of Nicholas Rowe, volume 1* (Routledge, 2017) and co-editor of *The Secret History in Literature, 1660–1820* (Cambridge, 2017).

Advisory Board

About the Series

Exploring connections between verbal and visual texts and the people, networks, cultures and places that engendered and enjoyed them during the long Eighteenth Century, this innovative series also examines the period's uses of oral, written and visual media, and experiments with the digital platform to facilitate communication of original scholarship with both colleagues and students.

Cambridge Elements ≡

Eighteenth-Century Connections

Elements in the Series

Printed in the United States
by Baker & Taylor Publisher Services

Printed in the United States
by Baker & Taylor Publisher Services